F&S

ARCHITECTURE INTERIORS LANDSCAPES

COLLAB- ORATIONS FERGUSON & SHAMAMIAN ARCHITECTS

TEXT BY DAVID MASELLO

FOREWORD BY MARGARET RUSSELL

DESIGN BY CHARLES CHURCHWARD

RIZZOLI
NEW YORK

New York · Paris · London · Milan

Previous spread:
Study alcove in a house
in Santa Monica.

This spread: Entrance
gallery of an apartment at
2 East 67th Street.

Following spread:
Winding stair in Aspen.

CONTENTS

FOREWORD

THE ESSENCE OF POWERFUL architecture is emotion. There's a certain romance to be found in following the evolution of a magnificent house from its inception all the way to completion. Perhaps an impromptu sketch on a scrap of paper sparks a concept, which develops through the detailed, methodical process of design, permits, construction, and layers of decoration, eventually coming to fruition in an elegant, beautifully realized home, one ready to be warmed by the personality, spirit, and joie de vivre of the people who live there. Tracing this creative path always makes my heart skip a beat, especially when it's that of a residence conceived in collaboration with the brilliant architectural team at Ferguson & Shamamian.

Though "collaboration" is not the first word one normally associates with world-class architects—as a longtime design editor I've often navigated talents whose buildings were dwarfed by the size of their egos—Ferguson & Shamamian truly stands apart. Fueled by a commitment not only to artistic excellence but to mindful collaboration, the firm has deftly conceived and built some of the most influential, high-octane residences of our time—from idyllic country estates, striking mountain retreats, and sun-splashed seaside compounds to fabled city apartments in buildings imbued with legend and pedigree.

Over the years, Ferguson & Shamamian has partnered both here and abroad on projects with a range of design talents—notably Victoria Hagan, Michael S. Smith, and Bunny Williams, whose exquisite interiors are showcased in this monograph, as well as those by Nina Campbell, Douglas Durkin, Jacques Grange, Timothy Haynes and Kevin Roberts, Brian Murphy of Parish-Hadley, Madeline Stuart, and Tino Zervudachi. The firm's relationship with Bunny Williams is particularly special, as she, Mark Ferguson, and Oscar Shamamian are all former protégés of Albert Hadley, sharing a common history at the iconic decorating firm Parish-Hadley. The two architects have noted that

their collaborative approach to projects was originally shaped by Parish-Hadley's decidedly client- and designer-centric mindset, a focus that was the antithesis of that embraced by most architecture firms of the time. Through early projects with Bunny and other Parish-Hadley colleagues, Mark and Oscar developed a firm grasp on the importance of scale and proportion in decor, the graceful flow of thoughtful room layouts, and the capacity of architecture to create a sense of comfort, ease, and living well within a space.

Though architects are commonly chided for sounding cerebral and obtuse when speaking with others, by the time they launched their own firm, Mark and Oscar were well-versed in a straightforward, client-friendly vocabulary. Their first project was a referral from Bunny Williams, who has collaborated with Ferguson & Shamamian on behalf of shared clients ever since. Working with them, Bunny says, "is an absolute joy. They have built some of the most beautiful new houses and transformed existing structures through what feel like seamless renovations. Their understanding of classical proportions, scale, details, and functionality—along with their amazing creativity—have resulted in extraordinary work."

Madeline Stuart, whose first collaboration with the firm is featured in these pages, readily admits, "It's not always easy; some architects can be imperious, and often designers fight to impose their own specific look onto an architect's approved plan. That's how you end up with a mishmash of stylistic influences." In contrast, though, for her the experience of working with the Ferguson & Shamamian team on an Italianate villa was "unbelievably gratifying because we shared a single vision and were unified in our approach."

"I never realized how extraordinarily practical and pragmatic Oscar and Mark are—possibly due to their work at Parish-Hadley, or maybe that's just who they are," says longtime collaborator Michael S. Smith. "They develop spaces that very much work for our clients, understanding how each room functions as part of the larger, cohesive whole. The team always brings a fresh eye to a project, and part of the joy and productivity of our work together is that not one of us is ever hesitant to propose what might sound like a crazy idea but could end up being brilliant.

"Oscar always makes me feel like I have a bigger box of crayons to color with," Michael says, "like I can run faster and jump higher because professionally I have a partner who helps me transform my ideas into three-dimensional reality. And he finds the same joy and excitement in the process that I do. Also, something surprising: I love that they are calm. No matter what happens—and sometimes things happen—they always remain calm. The entire team is seriously task-oriented and able to handle any surprises. It's a culture of calm."

Designer Tino Zervudachi, who partnered with Ferguson & Shamamian on the design and construction of his client's Connecticut estate, says, "I had worked with the firm before and appreciated their creativity, mindfulness, and focus; they look at everything in great detail, even the smallest elements of design."

Throughout this project, Tino observes, "There was a remarkable feeling that we were a family working together, sharing ideas and collaborating in the most profound way to create the very best for the client." He adds, "The firm's thoughtful, dedicated approach is rare, and it has helped to build an exceptional ongoing relationship between us, one that is based on complete trust."

"Ferguson & Shamamian's work always has a connection to the land and the light," says Victoria Hagan, who partners with the firm on a wide range of projects, both classic and contemporary, and has often created multiple residences for long-standing clients. "You don't need to explain why the light is so important to a room; they already know. They are incredibly thoughtful listeners and they look at each project from all perspectives—the architecture, the interiors, and the landscape—which is so integral to what we do." Victoria adds, "I always know I'm in good hands. My clients and I trust them. There's an undeniable level of confidence and trust that they're steering the ship exactly where it needs to go."

That resounding sense of trust is shared not only by Ferguson & Shamamian's roster of high-profile international clients but by its family of collaborative partners—from interior designers and landscape architects to builders, artisans, contractors, technology consultants, and tradespeople. Through stunning photography and intriguing storytelling, the selection of sublime projects featured in this book celebrates their collective expertise. But the core and foundation of each of the residences documented here remain the architecture—classically oriented structures conceived and built in a traditional idiom that is supremely relevant to modern life.

There is a relaxed elegance evident in even the most monumental Ferguson & Shamamian projects; the grandeur is subtle, not intimidating, and impeccable architectural details lend a refined sense of the past. Their volumes of space can seem unexpectedly intimate—authentic, with an absence of arrogance or bravado. The less formal, more understated houses in these pages radiate the warmth of hand-hewn surfaces and soothing textures, the play of sunlight on timeworn floors, the seamless weavings of indoors and out—of garden vistas and views of the sea. In truth, if the essence of Ferguson & Shamamian is revealed through the strength, beauty, and grace of these exceptional residences, the firm's legacy is defined by the book's fascinating supplement of elevations, renderings, working drawings, and site plans for the featured projects (pages 249–79). This artful addendum represents the architects' tools of communication and collaboration; it reflects the history and integrity of work well done, and a glorious foundation for the future.

—MARGARET RUSSELL, *January 2021*

INTRODUCTION

WE BELIEVE THE WORLD is held together by collaboration: effortless and difficult, simple and complex, and ever changing. The fourteen homes captured in this monograph represent the elaborate interplay between clients, architecture, interiors, landscape, and construction. These forces, among many others, come together and, through push and pull, create a house that is beautiful, comfortable, and functional for all who experience it.

It's easy to speak well of working with others in hindsight, but actually, teamwork can be complicated and success is never assured. Relying on others can be inspiring and energizing . . . and also messy. Great collaboration requires intensive work; difficult collaboration requires far more work.

During the process of creating a house or apartment, the design and construction teams must align thousands of times. Ideas, decisions, negotiations, problems, and solutions are influenced by everyone and everything, from tradespeople, artisans, and architectural review boards to tree root systems, gutter leaders, asbestos tests, molding profiles, culling marble in South America, and the size of a client's dinner plates.

While all architecture requires collaboration to some degree, it has become the bedrock of our firm through a combination of luck, practice, and muscle memory. To understand how this came to be, we should go back to our origins. Although we are both products of New Jersey, we are very different people from opposite poles of this great state. Mark grew up on a farm in South Jersey, eventually moving on to pursue architecture at Carnegie Mellon University and Princeton University. He married and moved to New York to start a family and his career. Oscar grew up in the North Jersey suburb of Englewood in the waning days of the 1970s before traveling a mere five miles to Columbia University, where he would spend eight years transforming from a young hellion to a designer and architect. Eventually, we found ourselves working together at Parish-Hadley, one of the world's most influential design firms.

At Parish-Hadley, we learned the art of suspending differences to achieve a common goal. Albert Hadley was unusually collaborative for a principal in a firm of such renown. He was a soft-spoken teacher and mentor who was interested in the development of the project and getting into the trenches with his designers. His "un-*Fountainhead*" notion of sharing ideas between architect and interior designer, and with everyone else for that matter, was the best method of teaching design—one not taught in graduate programs of architectural schools at the time. We shared the same open-mindedness and thrived on the ideas and expertise of each other and those around us. When we set out to form an architecture firm, we understood that success would require enormous effort, perseverance, and a high degree of collaboration. So collaborate we did. In our practice, we found a way of working together that has produced a body of work that looks like it is from one hand.

In the early days of Ferguson & Shamamian, our focus was to find as many projects as possible and keep our doors open. As the firm grew, we quickly learned that the most successful associations derive not only from the most qualified people, but also from those you enjoy being around. We realized that we were building an organization based on long-term relationships with our staff. Our mission became to create a firm where any employee could build an entire career and develop personally and professionally fulfilling relationships with colleagues. Central to that undertaking are our fundamental core values—excellence, integrity, curiosity, and collaboration. We strive to adhere to these ideas in interactions with all people. Regardless of position or role, we and our colleagues remind ourselves of these principles on a daily basis as we continually strengthen the framework on which our firm grows and matures.

Education, mentorship, and teaching are also vital to the foundation of our practice. We encourage everyone in the office to expand their sphere of influence by taking advantage of our relationships with organizations that promote and preserve the practice of traditional architecture and interior design; by mentoring peers; and by teaching other architects—a role Mark has taken to a new level as the dean of the School of Architecture and Planning at the Catholic University of America in Washington, D.C.

Given that over 40 percent of our staff of eighty have been with the firm for more than ten years, and that our leadership team of nine partners and principals has 217 combined years at the firm, we believe our foundation is strong. After thirty years working beside these dedicated and capable people, we are fortunate to find ourselves with nine leaders who work as a single unit to run the firm. We are humbled to see what was once a small atelier now becoming a multi-generational company.

Our ethos of surrounding ourselves with the most talented and collaborative people we could find became so ingrained in our firm's culture that it naturally expanded to include the many interior designers, land-scape designers, builders, artisans, and consultants with whom we have built decades-long relationships. This endeavor to design residences requires the imagination and the energy of many people, and we are fortunate to have associations with so many who share a piece of every project with us. Of course, it was both fascinating and terrifying to realize we had developed a unique business model dependent largely on people outside of the firm. In the beginning, we never imagined that when Bunny Williams—a great counselor to us at Parish-Hadley and still to this day—introduced us to our first client in 1988, we would complete over thirty projects with her, including eight with that first client. Nor that after we were somewhat thrown together with Victoria Hagan on an early project, Victoria would become one of our most trusted advocates and colleagues with whom we continue to work to achieve shared visions for our mutual clients.

Whether less is more or more is more, the architecture is in the details. Classical, vernacular, the purely decorative, and the minimal all find expression in the work.

And we certainly never could have foreseen when Michael S. Smith arrived at our first meeting in his casual West Coast attire that he would become one of the firm's most prolific and creative partners on over fifty projects, a most valued champion, and a friend. We are lucky to have them, and many others, to depend on.

Our clients are an equally essential part of this process. We count among our greatest accomplishments that we have been fortunate to work with over fifty clients who have returned—and continue to return—to build more than one residence with us. It's hard to believe that we are now building for several of their children. We're happy to report that we continue to grow with their grandchildren in mind. We'll be ready when the time comes!

All of this history, perseverance, and continual effort to surround ourselves with brilliantly talented and inspiring people over the past thirty-three years brings us to the reason for this book. Collaboration is our foundation, and it is expected of everyone at every level of a project. It is second nature for our leadership team after all of our years together, and it is up to the nine of us partners and principals, as well as our more experienced colleagues, to help others understand that this is the way we work. Ego has no place at the table. Everyone is given a chance to speak, to be heard, to contribute, to critique, and to learn. There is an expectation that everyone will be respectful, attentive, and responsive to every idea. In this environment, confidence builds and individual talents naturally emerge; all members of our team learn to acknowledge what they can and

cannot do by themselves. In some settings, "design by committee" can lead to mediocrity; however, with vision, integrity, and practice, the right leadership can guide a talented team to remarkable creativity and excellence. We believe every one of our projects is the better for it, as is our firm.

Our first monograph, *New Traditional Architecture*, was a look back over twenty years of projects and the promise of a continuum of beautiful buildings. Realizing how much that book depended on decoration and landscape to present each residence in its environment, and how many of those clients came to us through interior designers, it was only natural that this next book would be about the many artists who convene to make these extraordinary residences together.

Our firm has been described as adaptable. We believe this representation results from being grounded in principle, yet perceptive and open to seeing the value and beauty in many different things. The pages that follow illustrate a vast range of projects. All are unique. Whether a villa, a barn, or a penthouse, we find each equally challenging and interesting. Perhaps most fascinating, however, is understanding that scores of people—each with particular internal expectations at the beginning of a project—come together to support and challenge one another in the pursuit of creating a portrait of the client, and not one of themselves. In our practice, we've realized the only way to attain this level of teamwork is by truly understanding and accepting that collaboration is not a finite achievement, but a practice that we continually strive to improve upon and develop every day.

—*MARK FERGUSON AND OSCAR SHAMAMIAN, April 2021*

STORIED PAST

The homeowners wanted their East Hampton house to replicate a venerable architectural style typical of the region and its history. But then they decided to write their own story.

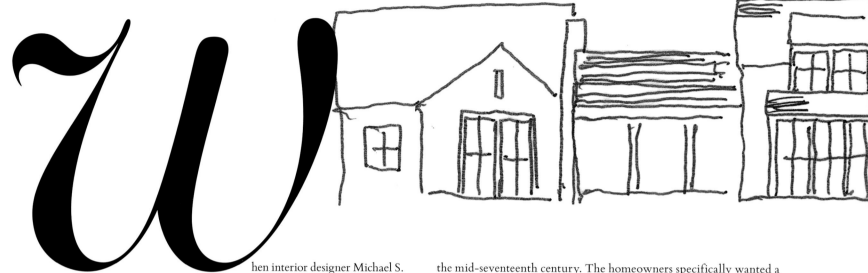

𝒲hen interior designer Michael S. Smith met with the husband-and-wife homeowners to assess a long, narrow parcel of East Hampton land, the ocean roiling at one end and a quiet lane at the other, they talked as if they were planning to make a movie. Smith, who has worked with the clients on numerous projects, admits that he thinks cinematically. So much so that Smith is able to envision exactly how a still-unbuilt house occupies the land, what its façades reveal, and what the rooms should contain and convey, in terms of both decor and architectural detail. For Smith, it's as much about the furnishings as it is about the way the beams should appear weathered by age.

But because the making of a house involves multiple parties—architects, interior designers, landscape architects, homeowners, masons—everyone, at certain points, has a starring role. The idea for this house, which has two distinct identities, front and back, began with a sketch the homeowner made on a sheet of notebook paper. It was a simple, even crude drawing, but it contained the seed of the story of this house, with a plot sufficiently compelling to propel Ferguson & Shamamian, Smith, and landscape architect Arne Maynard to realize a finished residence.

That casually drawn floorplan revealed a one-and-a-half-story main house with two bedrooms, executed as a modified saltbox—the kind of home found throughout the Hamptons, a locale first settled by the English in the mid-seventeenth century. The homeowners specifically wanted a house that appeared modest in scale at its approach. But they also wanted room for guests and for their children and grandchildren. A guest residence, situated closer to the main road, would need to include six bedrooms, as well as public rooms, including a gym and an open kitchen. So the building program called for something both grand and modest at the same time— in keeping with the metaphor, an epic movie that told a quiet story. The narrative of a converted barn located close to the land was developed. In talking to the interior designer and architects, the homeowners kept using words like "cozy," "warm," and "homey" to describe the effect and mood they sought.

As for the saltbox, it's an inherently appealing style—a kind of golden retriever breed of architecture, curbside-friendly, symmetrical, a definitive American example, uncontroversial, with an ability to contextualize regardless of its neighbors. This particular house, however, based on the local Amagansett farmhouse type, is not without its controversies. Walk to the rear façade and the modified saltbox gives way suddenly and dramatically to contemporary. Where the front elevation is marked by handsome gabled dormers, multipaned double-hung windows, massive brick chimneys, and evenly spaced narrow clapboards, the back is a different house entirely. Walking the width of the house is akin to coursing a time tunnel.

Previous spread: East Hampton dunes.

Above: An early sketch of the rear façade by Oscar Shamamian. *Below*: The long, narrow site from the ocean and dunes (*left*) to the main house, gardens, orchards, and guesthouse.

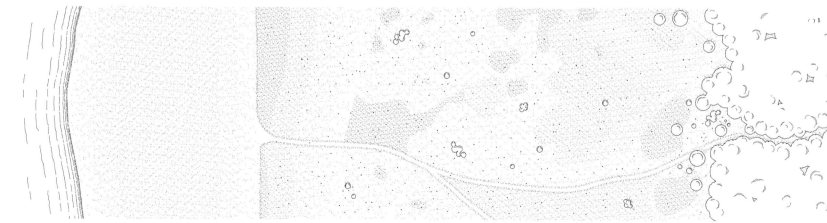

Stand back far enough from a series of undulating sand dunes and the breadth of the back of the house comes into view, as it nearly fills the width of the lot. From this vantage, the windows appear blown out; absent muntins, the dormers dispense with their peaks and become shallower shed-style ones. Most conspicuous, though, are those walls of large triple-hung windows, designed in such a way that when two sashes are raised, a person is able to walk through to the outside, as if the fenestration has all along been an open, transparent doorway. The precedent for the form can be found at Thomas Jefferson's Monticello and other houses. Historical precedents often calm any qualms a homeowner might have over building something radically new. Those windows not only define the rear elevation, but also reflect their climatic function. Hurricanes are no longer uncommon phenomena in the Hamptons, and to ensure that the glass could withstand gale-force winds, the windows were tested in a laboratory—with two-by-fours hurled at them at sixty miles per hour.

Inside, too, the cinematic quality of the house quickly reveals itself. Vigorous timber beams and floor joists that cross the barnlike space of the main house feature notches to suggest there was once a second floor. But as in all works of fiction, truth is irrelevant, and there never was another level. From inception, Ferguson & Shamamian, in concert with Smith, sought to create the impression of an old local farmhouse to which wings

had been added over the centuries, floors removed, barn areas converted to living quarters. The architects embarked on detailed studies of the framing methods of Colonial-era houses in the region to see exactly how and where the joists and beams were located and where they would register notches and grooves. So exacting is Smith in creating the right feel and period details that the timbers used in the interiors are distressed sufficiently to seem as if they were salvaged from a structure built in the eighteenth century. But as the Ferguson & Shamamian team says, with jocularity, Smith's influence is such that he could likely coax the wood timbers themselves, by force of will, to age to the proper look.

The main dwelling is configured, essentially, as a one-and-a-half-story box at the middle with two meandering wings, one punctuated with stone at the end. The guesthouse "barn" was designed to be less symmetrical. The stonework by master mason Bruce O'Brien is a strong subplot of the story line of the house. It's as if a farmer who tended the land generations ago had built a series of stone buildings on the property—some of which were taken down so as to repurpose the stones for other structures, while others were used for their intended purposes and have weathered naturally over the centuries. None of these stone buildings could be mistaken for a ruin, but they hint at a state far in the future that makes them all the more precious and appreciated now.

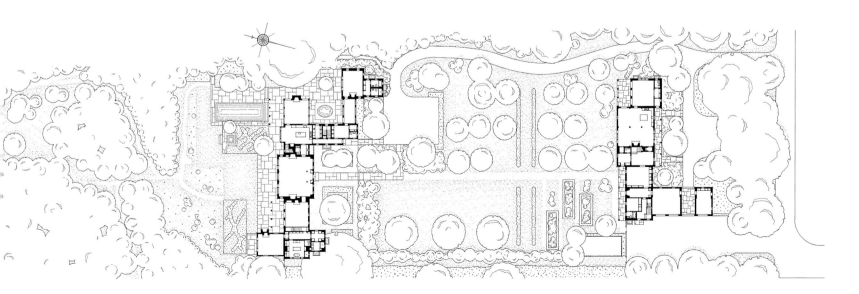

Previous spread: A pebbled pathway leads to the main house. Landscape architect Arne Maynard included grapevines as part of the orchard and replanted three existing magnolia trees, pruning them into dome-like masses.

Opposite: A quiet moment within the layered landscape. *Below, left to right*: A single granite lintel attests to the use of traditional masonry construction, expertly realized by stonemason Bruce O'Brien; four-inch clapboard on the guesthouse references eighteenth-century local buildings.

There's yet another plot-driven story line attached to this house, that of the landscape, one that has been written by the prolific landscape architect Arne Maynard. As he envisions it, long ago, before the arrival of this house, guesthouse, and the property's ancillary elements, a fictional farmer who lived here cultivated fruit orchards, fields of potatoes, and even pumpkin patches. Remnants of that centuries-old agricultural lineage of the far East End of Long Island remain, and Maynard hoped to honor it. He wanted this newly tamed land to seem as if it had played a role in the original agricultural roots of East Hampton—that a farmer, long ago, had to relinquish the bounty of the land, let the orchards go fallow, and allow the sand dunes to run up and into the yard.

Maynard is English and he understands the shape and topography of British medieval planting fields, an effect he achieved here with imperfect grids of crabapple trees planted in furrows that replicate the ancient English method and undulate across the land. Ridges and furrows, vines trained along old fence posts, massive beech and magnolia trees, gnarled yew trees, and box hedges all point to generations of tenders of the land—though time has been kind enough to create a handsome choreography of plantings. As Maynard sums up his story of this property, "It's a timeless landscape. It won't age. It will become more mature, the trees more gnarly, and it will all continue to feel even more settled, part of the landscape as a whole."

From the start, the homeowners were aware of Smith's, Ferguson & Shamamian's, Maynard's, and O'Brien's abilities to evoke the human hand inside, outside, and on the land. The cinematic appeal of the finished house is that it appears to be of the past, but developed over time in a unique way, the result of a consortium of present-day imaginations.

Previous spread: Joist pockets in the timbers of the great room suggest a former floor that had been removed.

Above: Outside the dining pergola, the pool extends lengthwise toward the ocean.
Opposite: Full-height triple-hung windows maximize views to the ocean.

Following spread: A metal-and-glass wall separates the library from the second floor, allowing
light from a dormer above.

Throughout the property,
the architecture and landscape
reinforce the concept of an
eighteenth-century farm that
has been lived in for generations
and transformed over time.

Following spread: Barn doors and
mature fruit trees emphasize
the appearance of the guesthouse
as a converted barn.

FLUENT IN SPANISH

While Spanish-Mediterranean is not a novel architectural style in Southern California, here it assumes a new and pronounced accent.

Previous spread: Every coffer
of the rakishly angled
dining room ceiling contains
a stenciled pattern.

Opposite: A dining loggia with
view to the canyon beyond.
Left: The thickness of the walls
is emphasized by a splayed
jamb at an arched window.

Following spread, left: Spanish
features—some salvaged,
some designed anew—create a
sense of place. *Following spread,
right*: The entry features steel-
and-glass doors between
the courtyard and the stair hall.

o one would mistake Santa
Monica for Spain's Andalusia, yet a townscape evocative of the Iberian
locale can be recreated in Southern California and seamlessly fit in. As
one enters the red-tiled courtyard of this home, with a lotus leaf–strewn
fountain gurgling at its center, the sensation of having journeyed to another
land is immediate. While context is a dynamic of residential architecture
in that a house should honor its neighbors, so, too, is it valid for architects to
create something sufficiently evocative of another place that a visitor can
feel transported there.

So convincing is this residence of a townscape one might encounter in
Andalusia that its architectural elements, inside and out, seem authentic,
as if imported from abroad. From select vantages on this steep site, with
views onto the Riviera Country Club, elevations of the house assume the
look of entire streetscapes. A pastiche of parts works to evoke a fantastic
storybook version of Spain. The sharply tapering lines of an outdoor
fireplace reference Moorish motifs, while its chimney is topped with a
miniaturized double-arched bell tower, a form found in Spanish villages.
Orthogonal wings and ells evoke a rustic white-stucco farmhouse. Some
elevations are punctuated with wrought-iron Juliet *balcones*. Far below,
the arches of a stone pool house vault rhythmically across the yard, not
unlike a Roman aqueduct. And in one of the house's more dramatic
moments, a parabolic window traces a wall of the family room.

The Ferguson & Shamamian team points to that moment of fenestration
as not only an actual window but also one that offers a view into the past,
namely to Wallace Neff, the influential Southern California architect
of the 1920s and '30s. Situated as it is in the rustic portion of the house,
the window is illusionary, as if its presence indicates a restoration of a
dwelling that has been evolving. It gives the stucco-and-wood structure

the feel of one whose various parts have been stitched together over a
long period of time.

Los Angeles does have an architectural history, despite much of the
region's relative newness. At this property especially, there is a past to
acknowledge. Prior to Ferguson & Shamamian's structure, another Spanish-
Mediterranean house stood here. Back in 1927, when Santa Monica was a
sleepy seaside town yet to be discovered by surfers, skateboarders, and stars,
Louis B. Mayer, the movie mogul, built his home on this site (period
photos reveal it was the sole structure in the neighborhood). In its day, it
was an elegant home, somber in mood and introspective, as most of its
rooms looked inward rather than outward to the ravines and scrolling
profile of mountains. For many years, the current homeowners lived
in—and loved—that original home, having raised their children there.
But when the owners commissioned the architects, as well as interior
designer Michael S. Smith, with whom they have worked for more than
twenty years, to revamp that house, something was discovered that
changed the course of action and would haunt the homeowners.

While new finishes were being conceived inside and architectural
elements outside, it was discovered that the house lacked the structural
support required in earthquake-prone locales such as Southern California.
Although everyone on the design team, as well as the homeowners,
had initially wanted to restore the house rather than erect a new one, upon
learning the news about the foundation the owners immediately opted
to demolish the existing house. Indeed, the wife was apparently so distressed
by the literal hollowness of her house (with its lack of rebar) that she
started sleeping with sneakers on, ready to bolt at the first tremor.

Any structure dating from the 1920s in Los Angeles, particularly if it
has movie-industry lineage, is considered historic—though not necessarily

Right: A parabolic window, divided with narrow muntins, references the architecture of Wallace Neff while also being decidedly contemporary. *Below*: A segmental arch with an overscaled splayed jamb separates the main bedroom from the sitting room.

architecturally significant. Such was the case with the Mayer house, though it took considerable lobbying by all parties to convince various Santa Monica agencies and councils to comply with the idea of tearing it down. Sometimes architects must read political blueprints, too, and Ferguson & Shamamian found itself immersed in the minutiae of the negotiations to replace the house. The initial impetus, and enthusiasm, for renovating the existing house was replaced with a directive to build anew.

So keen were the homeowners to embrace all things Spanish that they took a trip to Spain with Smith to find just the right details to complement their daily lives in California. The Ferguson & Shamamian team was well aware that various elements of decor would be arriving from Spain—paintings of conquistadores, Spanish Baroque cabinets, painted tiles—but alert, too, to the fact that as architects they needed to express an abundance of Spanish-Mediterranean detailing without compromising the integrity of the house. Just as the talented Smith wished to express the individual voice of each room, so did the architects wish to articulate the overall image of the house.

The 12,000-square-foot house is sited on the land as a main block with a long perpendicular arm traversing the slope. The pool house and pool are sited at the bottom of a steep grade, while a separate building for a garage and media room is positioned near the main residence. This geometric arrangement on a complicated topographical site has resulted in a house that appears much smaller than it is—a desire, from inception, of the homeowners. Where many of the rooms in the original house looked onto internal courtyards, this new residence captures natural light and embraces the views beyond. The obsessively in-control Louis B. Mayer had built an unadorned, boxy house, decidedly formal in its arrangement and scale; the current homeowners wanted, instead, a layering of textures, elements of contemporary architecture, and a casual feel and atmosphere.

Indicative of his penchant for thematic detail, Smith purchased for the dining room six seventeenth-century paintings of conquistadores. He found them at a Christie's auction of furnishings from the estate of Duarte Pinto Coelho (1923–2010), the famous Portuguese designer and bon vivant of his day. Coincidentally, Trujillo, the town in Spain where Coelho had a vacation house, was the same area from which explorers had come to the New World of California. Rather than hanging the artworks on the dining room walls, however, Smith had them embedded in the walls, flush with the surfaces. As a result, the nearly life-size, helmeted figures appear as if painted in situ, akin to frescoes—again, the kind of detail endemic to a house that has evolved over centuries.

Typical of a Ferguson & Shamamian and Smith collaboration is the design of a distinctive ceiling. In the dining room, deeply recessed coffers are set at a 45-degree angle—a bias that serves as an intriguing foil to the 90-degree rectilinear paneling on the walls. The rakishly angled ceiling adds yet another texture, an animating element of drama, to a room already infused with the narrative of portraits that depict a Spanish colonial past.

Most interior designers embrace the concept that what a house announces at the entry should be echoed throughout all of the rooms. Such is the case here, with an arresting combination of structure and style that greets visitors. Upon entering the house through a contemporary multipaned steel-and-glass doorway, one encounters, simultaneously, vibrantly patterned Spanish tilework rising halfway up the walls, akin to wainscoting, as well as a bold staircase seemingly floating in air. The staircase's oak treads are fully articulated as they rise and make a swift 180-degree turn on their run up to the second floor. What looks structurally miraculous is the result of concealed steel supports. While the staircase's sculptural form may echo forms found in Spanish-Mediterranean–style houses, the design is wholly original. Another practical reason for its floating form, however, is that it conveniently snakes past and above a large window that allows natural light to stream into the foyer.

What the staircase emphasizes is that this is a house of details—found throughout every room, in the gardens and the courtyards, and at the bottom of the hill where the pool terrace is connected to the house through an underground corridor. Though probably not as dramatic as the discoveries of the conquistadores, surprises await those who tour the house. Such is the daily experience for the homeowners, who claim to experience awe every time they enter. Life is good in Andalusia and California.

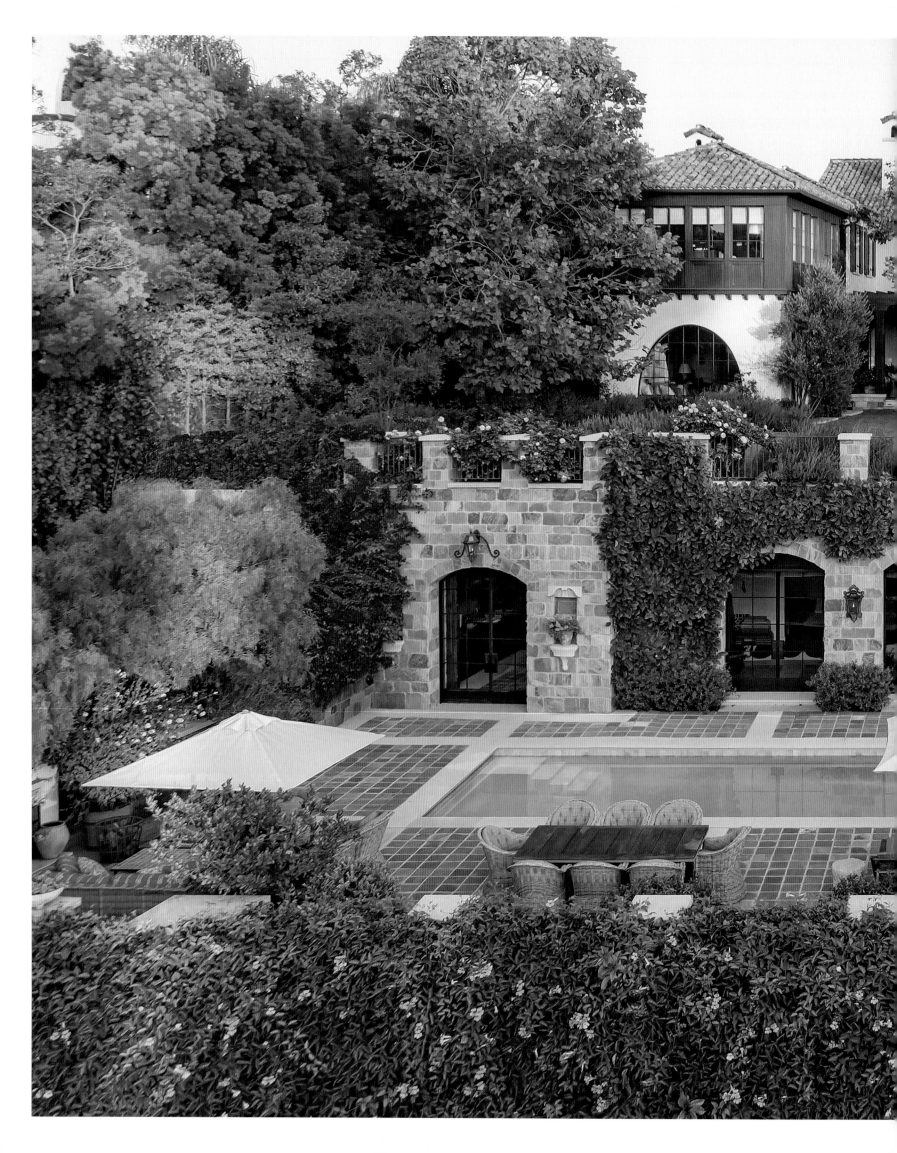

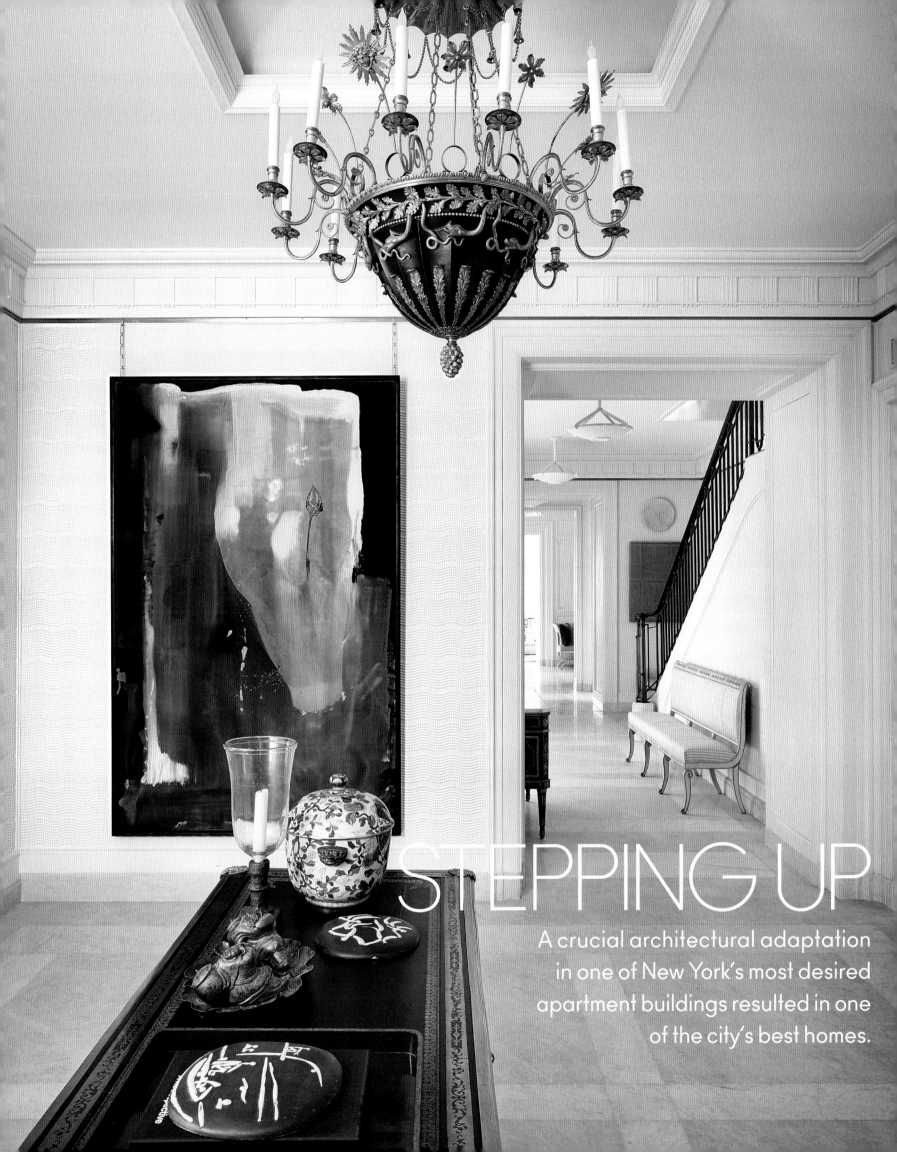

STEPPING UP

A crucial architectural adaptation
in one of New York's most desired
apartment buildings resulted in one
of the city's best homes.

*W*hen one of Manhattan's most coveted duplex apartments, in one of the most coveted buildings, came on the market, a parade of potential clients, architects, and real estate brokers marched through the space. It was a space everyone wanted, but couldn't have. At least, not in the way they wanted to occupy it.

The longtime former owners had preferred to keep what was originally two separate duplexes virtually disconnected so that they could use one apartment for entertaining and the other as a private residence. While each expansive apartment had its own signature curved stair, the principal means of getting from one unit to the other was through an awkward detour into and around an elevator vestibule. The challenge was to devise a way to integrate the two apartments, but one potential buyer after another concluded that the two parts could not be unified gracefully. As a result, the Park Avenue residence remained on the market for an extended period.

That is, until Oscar Shamamian and interior designer Michael S. Smith arrived with the clients and their real estate broker. Shamamian, on a hunch, came prepared to investigate and to confirm whether any of the documented encumbrances actually existed. Shamamian asked one of his project architects to explore under one of the existing stairs with a flashlight and tape measure to discern whether there were any impediments to joining the two apartments. Through an access door under the stair, the team discovered that the original plans incorrectly located plumbing pipes in between the apartments, a discovery that proved the stair could in fact be breached to combine the two apartments.

But the solution for linking the apartments called for committing a heretical action in New York: eliminating a significant curved stair in favor of a side-mounted,

Previous spread, left: One original Candela-designed staircase was reclad with perla venata quartzite; the new stair metalwork is by La Forge De Style. *Previous spread, right*: A view of the apartment's long enfilade, from the entry gallery past the new stair to the living room.

Opposite and right: Féau et Cie paneling in the dining room was inspired by Jean-Michel Frank's interpretation of Louis XIV–style boiserie for a 1930s apartment in Paris.

straight one. The client still speaks of the two holy grails of Manhattan apartments—curved stairs and a Central Park view—and his willingness to sacrifice one of them. "No one would even think to eliminate a [Rosario] Candela staircase," the homeowner says as a way to remind himself of his bold decision. He and his wife now live in one of the city's grandest homes, a twenty-two-room showplace Shamamian refers to as "one of the best results of one of the very best collaborations we've ever done." The decision freed the team's imagination and gave them license to be as courageous on all subsequent design elements. And while Shamamian cites people as the engines of that process, he can't help but acknowledge, too, the role that curiosity, a flashlight, and a tape measure played.

Although the apartment was gutted and the original floorplan largely recreated, this shift in the staircase's position resulted in the apartment's most notable feature: a seventy-five-foot-long uninterrupted corridor that cuts through each level. Light pours in now from each side, with the views of Central Park even more pronounced. Many Park Avenue apartments, despite their pedigree—and this Candela building is the most royal blue blood on the street—can be dark, with the rooms feeling internalized. It is also possible, according to hearsay, that this resulting hallway is the longest enfilade on the avenue.

The clients have worked for more than twenty-five years with both the interior designer, Michael S. Smith, and Ferguson & Shamamian on multiple homes—in Manhattan, Montecito, Malibu, East Hampton—and they wanted this new apartment to feel cosmopolitan and glamorous. That narrative made sense given the architecture of the building itself, a restrained, elegant, confident structure on the avenue. Unusual for Candela, the nineteen-story apartment house built in 1930 embodies a

53

particularly refined, streamlined version of the Art Deco style. Massive bronze windows punctuate the façades, and walking into the building's lobby is akin to wading into a still pool of polished marble.

The architects eagerly responded to the clients' and Smith's desire for a quiet sense of sophistication. Where possible, the architects raised ceilings as far as they could, stepping them to emphasize verticality and as a way to add visual flourishes. Most clients of this caliber want their walls to be left unadorned, absent elaborate paneling or textures, in order to better display their art and prefer instead to have the ceilings and floors be more architectural. Here, it was the reverse, with the clients willing to hang their Matisses and other artworks on walls that could be considered works of art as well.

Smith responded to this decision by gilding certain ceilings with a reflective treatment, notably in the bar, sunroom, and breakfast room. The wife's dressing room is silver leaf so convincing that one might think it needs regular polishing, but it never tarnishes. Smith refers to this treatment of the ceilings and walls as a way of "dematerializing" them, adding a greater optical dimension to the rooms.

Walls and floors play up their materiality with every effort made to find their sources. The project's principal designer traveled to Brazil to source stone slabs, while Smith toured Parisian warehouses and commissioned Féau et Cie to create five rooms of extraordinary French paneling. The previous owners had created a screening room for which the clients had no use. Smith ingeniously transformed the large area into a family room, a space the husband claims "blows away everything else in the apartment." Smith covered the room's walls with woven-raffia panels hand-stenciled in henna-colored patterns. Not every large room needs to seem large. The prosaic material on the walls makes the space more intimate by visually reducing its volume.

The work in the apartment involved a dream team of artisans and craftspeople—artists such as Miriam Ellner

Below, top to bottom: Original staircase prior to demolition, and reconceived as a straight flight of stairs. *Right*: Restored original bronze doors in the living room provide access to a balcony with views of southern Manhattan.

Opposite: His study is defined by Féau et Cie paneling and a lacquered ceiling. *Above*: Details of objects, finishes, and accessories chosen by interior designer Michael S. Smith, in concert with the clients.

Following spread: The hand-stenciled woven-raffia wall treatment in the family room stands out amid a beveled ceiling and flat decorative pilasters.

and Nancy Lorenz, along with decorative painters, gilders, plasterers, floor finishers, and stone workers—who worked for years to deliver one of the most gloriously detailed apartments in New York.

It's an axiom in architecture that successful projects require passionate clients. Ferguson & Shamamian emphasizes that these clients not only love good design, but also the process leading to good design. Given the impressive repertoire of projects the clients have built with Ferguson & Shamamian and Smith over the decades, the architects were aware that this project represented something especially ambitious and visionary for the couple. By purchasing an apartment of this scale and legacy, it was clear the clients wanted to make a new statement in their lives. This apartment had presented a seemingly unsolvable problem, but it has since been unified into a singular home, one that exactly reflects the clients' decision to lead a new life in a new place.

Left and above: A serene hall outside the main bedroom suite, with hidden doors for storage.

Following spread: Two views of the main bedroom. At right, in order to achieve a higher ceiling, a series of calculated gradual shallow steps manages the transition between the balconies above and the edge of the building setback.

Page 66: Her dressing room doors feature painted glass panels by Miriam Ellner. *Page 67*: The bar with mica walls and caplain gold–leaf woodwork and ceiling.

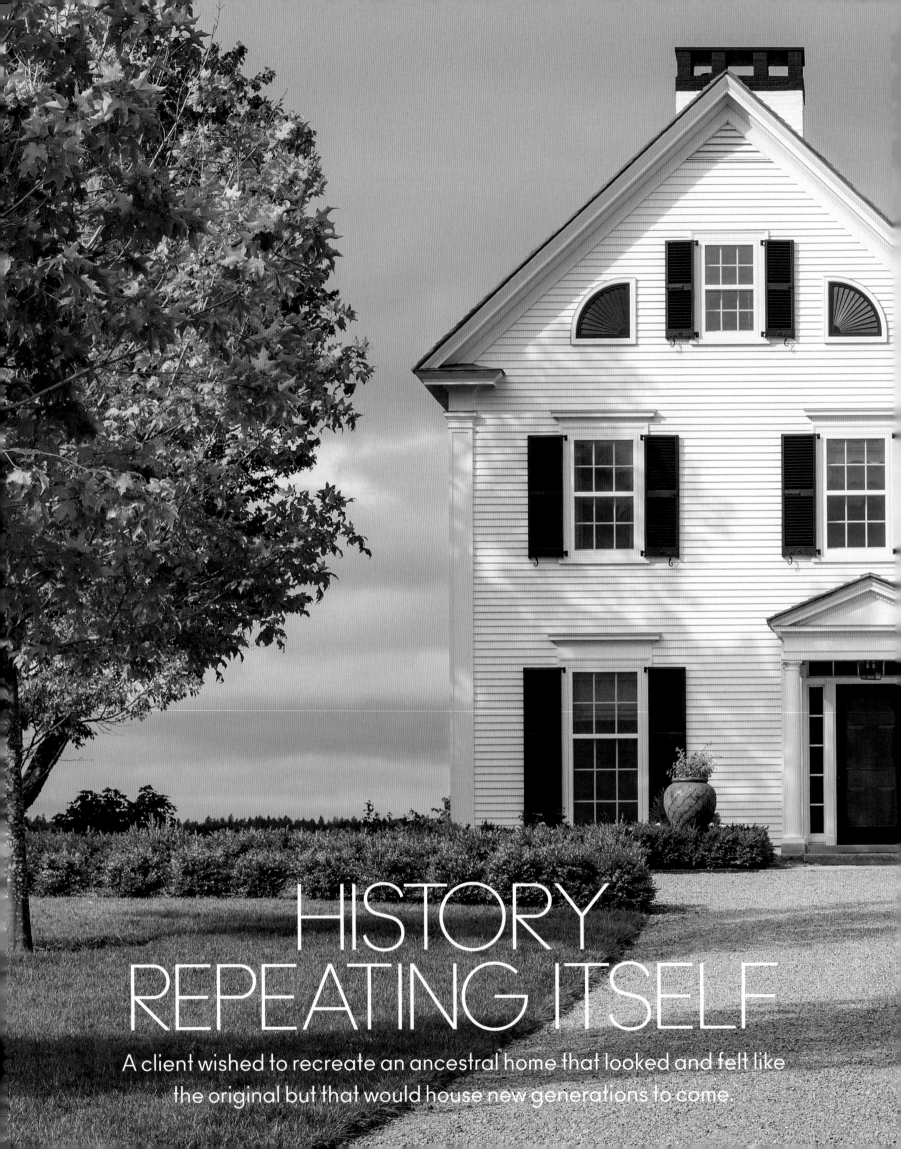

HISTORY REPEATING ITSELF

A client wished to recreate an ancestral home that looked and felt like the original but that would house new generations to come.

Previous spread: The front door was relocated to the right side of the entry to accommodate a staircase. Unlike before, the driveway now aligns with the front door.

Left: When one arrives from the water, the shoreline, main house, and pool house come into view.
Below: A bird's-eye pencil rendering explains the interlocking arrangement of the main house, pool house, pool, and gardens.

*W*hen this house was being built, certain procedures were hidden from the homeowners. While the couple knew what was taking place, he, in particular, didn't want to see it. So the Ferguson & Shamamian team, the contractor and builders, the landscape designer, the interior designer, even local townspeople and neighbors, purposely withheld information. It's not easy to keep matters from a man who is among America's most successful businessmen and philanthropists. While the homeowners had made the brave decision—after settling the matter with some twenty-five other members of the family trust—to tear down the ancestral house and replace it, sentimentality threatened to overwhelm them.

The new house was to be, in many ways, virtually identical to the residence that had stood on a Downeast Maine island since the late nineteenth century. The new residence would replicate visually that old frame dwelling, but the new version would be taller; there would be modern plumbing, of course (the original house had no

71

Opposite: Along the new winding driveway, a break in the trees reveals the breadth of the cove. *Below*: Abutting the long meadow and abandoned apple orchard near the entrance to the property, the maintenance complex resembles farm buildings around a central courtyard.

Following spread: Beyond the porte cochere lies a trellised arbor allée linking the pool and gardens.

indoor showers), new wings would expand its footprint, and outbuildings would arise on the 350-acre waterfront, through which new hiking and biking trails would be cut.

More importantly, the house would *almost* occupy the very site on which the first structure had stood—but with a shift of twelve feet to the north. The reason for the move involved saving a particular tree, beneath the limbs of which years of family picnics had taken place. As the homeowners' interior designer, Nina Campbell, later remarked, "Anybody who moves a house to save a tree should get an award."

However, while one unique tree was saved, others had to be cut down. The client stipulated that during demolition, no images should be shared with him, especially not of the removal of a dozen sugar maples that his grandparents had planted. Losing these trees was especially hard for him; their removal caused an emotional wounding. But ultimately, he accepted everything that came with his decision to build a new home evocative of the old one that would carry forward for generations to come. The old house had succumbed to its age; the new one would last far into the future. Here would be a different kind of history repeating itself—certainly a more enduring version of the past.

The clients had also emphasized to Ferguson & Shamamian that they wanted the new residence to feel as if a person who had been away from it for a few years would discover upon returning that little had changed—that the views were almost the same, that some of the old family furniture had simply been repurposed, and that the very DNA of the dwelling, as if it had been an actual living thing that housed generations of living family, had been replicated.

The husband is a homeowner for whom the smallest details, some no bigger than a pebble, matter. While he admits to owning the largest spread of land in the area and one of its largest residences, he remained keenly attuned to such matters as gravel. He speaks still of choosing gravel for the driveway based on how it would look when wet and how it would sound when walked upon or when car tires crunched on it. He insisted on a wireless neon sign spelling out DEVIL'S HIDEOUT (the name of the property's private nightclub, sited where the homeowner's boyhood treehouse, of the same name, once stood). He anchors his boats in the cove so that upon awakening, with his head still on the pillow, he can see them bobbing in the water. And he talks still about wanting to move lanterns

in the pool house one and three-quarter inches so as to better illuminate the food that is served there at a dinner.

What would have been a challenging dynamic for some architects, this client's careful attention to the most minute of details, became instead a fun call to arms. The architects speak admirably of the client's perfectionism—aligned with their own—not as a difficult trait, but rather as an inspiration and challenge. In fact, Ferguson & Shamamian felt compelled to heighten the drama and detailing of the house beyond the client's stipulations. For instance, the architects surprised him by designing custom weather vanes for buildings on the property. For the roof of a garage that occupies the site of the client's grandfather's landing strip, they created a weather vane in the shape of a small prop plane. Portions of the demolished house were salvaged and stored in a nearby warehouse, chiefly as a way, by reference, to faithfully produce new, more sound versions. Some of the original cabinets, mantels, even glass doorknobs were preserved as models based on which better versions were made from the same materials. And as a strategy for keeping construction to an eighteen-month schedule, actual portions of the new house were assembled off-site and brought to the property later.

The house is infused with a sense of both whimsy and import. Nina Campbell was entrusted with the task of introducing a particular shade of lavender into her elegant room designs. The color was a favorite of the client's grandfather; the more often the hue appears in everything from sofas, blankets, and ottomans to the client's own socks he puts on every day, the more that ancestor is honored on a daily basis. He even had the nightclub done mostly in that color; it is a space that is accessed through a hidden, lavender-painted British phone booth, not unlike a disguised entrance to a period speakeasy. The client wishes, too, to emphasize that the lavender is one of the colors of his alma mater and appears also in the logo of his company. He talks often about the new house being a Technicolor version of the old.

Like many Ferguson & Shamamian projects, this one takes on a cinematic quality, an effect accomplished in large part by landscape designer Deborah Nevins. As a result of her work, the property now presents itself with an unfolding story line. When conceiving the landscaping, the homeowner took everyone on a lengthy walk through the land, pointing out the locale of his boyhood treehouse, where fertile orchards once

Opposite: The playhouse stair. *Above*: In the office, a newly designed mantelpiece
incorporates a stone surround salvaged from the original living room fireplace. Cabinet doors are
recreations based on millwork found in the former house.

Following spread: The pocket doors of the pool house open fully to the pool terrace, a center of daily activity.
From the chaise longues, there are unobstructed views across the pool and lawn to the water.

flourished, and certain trees that held memories. The walk proved fruitful for all parties, especially for Nevins. Where the arrival to the original house had once been a straight shot through woods, there is now a pronounced choreography whose elements include a winding drive past a farm, orchards, water views coming into and out of focus, a patch of woods, a stone bridge, and, finally, venerable trees leading to the front entrance of the house.

Yet, despite the scale of the main house (some 20,000 square feet) and the many ancillary buildings, notably a playhouse with bowling lanes, a squash court, and the nightclub (with its own costume room), the complex appears modest in scale. No building, no room, no natural element feels outsized. Some elderly guests and family members who remember the original dwelling express a sense of déjà vu while sitting on some of the original furniture that was retained and gazing out on the familiar views. For them, it's as if nothing has changed, though they know everything has. For young guests and family members, this house represents a new start for the future.

The client continues to express awe at the result of everyone's labors. Even now, he says of—and to—the Ferguson & Shamamian team: "I live in a painting that, together, we have brought to life." He speaks, too, as a de facto philosopher of domestic family life: "A gathering place for one's family that brings together the past, the present and the dreams for the future, that is the true definition of one's lifework—and that is the definition of success."

Left: Landscape designer Deborah Nevins surrounded a dining pergola with lush plantings. *Above*: On a pathway leading to the playhouse, a pedestrian bridge straddling a stream is one of several examples of whimsical landscape features.

Clockwise from top left: The pool house pergola overlooks the firepit and cove beyond; the family room incorporates the homeowner's favorite lavender; the stairway is an expanded version of the one found in the old house and includes a decorative flourish; the pool house and pool are seen from the breakfast room.

Previous spread, left: From a porch, a descending sash allows for unencumbered access to the lawn. *Previous spread, right*: The playhouse is equipped with a variety of attractions, including two bowling lanes in a room evocative of a stable, as viewed from the nighttime lounge.

Left: In the nightclub, located inside the playhouse, LED lights behind a decorative cove can be changed to suit any mood. *Right*: A copper canopy marks the front door of the playhouse.

Following spread: Tucked away in the woods where the homeowner's childhood treehouse once perched, a grownup playhouse now stands. A new swing hangs where one has always been.

WASHED ASHORE

A Nantucket house, situated high above the coastline, stands out from the calm sea of neighboring residences, while also blending in.

*t*he waters off Nantucket have their hazards—unpredictable currents, riptides, the occasional great white. On land, requirements to preserve Nantucket's unique character and authentic sense of place could seem hazardous as well.

On the island, all proposed construction must pass review by the Nantucket Historic District Commission (HDC), a process that is often daunting to owners and their design team. The HDC guidelines stipulate the selection of exterior paint colors, appropriate front doors, building materials, windows, architectural features, and the size of a house—directives that keep Nantucket harmonious and beautiful. While architects may need to relinquish control of the exterior, those rules do not apply to the interior. Thus, while residential restraint and modesty are the prevailing aesthetic on the exterior, many of Nantucket's architectural surprises are best seen not from the curb but from the threshold.

This gray-shingled residence does have an authentic and rigorous demeanor on the outside, one that is largely hidden until you've turned off the street and negotiated the winding driveway. The house's real design surprises await beyond the front door. Ferguson & Shamamian, interior designer Douglas Durkin, and the enlightened clients created a house that both fits into its landscape and stands out from it. While it took many meetings with the HDC to study the house and ensure that it met the stringent requirements, in the end, this process proved freeing—akin, perhaps, to metered, rhymed poetry, in the sense that rules can allow for more creative results.

Despite its dense site, with neighboring houses close by, the house is positioned in such a way as to provide privacy and sanctuary. Another key design directive was to ensure that every façade had its own identity. Here, the street façade begins with the modest guesthouse that meets the curb—a small cottage, punctuated with six-over-six double-hung windows, a shed dormer, and less formal detailing, indicating the building's place in the hierarchy of the property. As one passes through a pair of wooden gates, anchored by roughly hewn stone pillars, the main residence comes into view, a house defined by well-balanced gabled wings, a four-window dormer, and a recessed, columned entrance porch. The rear of the house presents another handsome face, with its asymmetrical gable, an element typical of a Shingle-style house, only here the elevation also assumes a classical language, dressed with a colonnade. The pool house façade presents yet another face, one that appears to contain a second level, given its three projecting dormers. However, as one enters the open-air shed, the building presents itself as a vaulting loftlike space, the windows atop filling with light at night as if they are rooms within the structure.

As much as the house itself makes multiple architectural statements, so, too, does the landscaping. Landscape designer Julie Jordin speaks about "the tension between the house's traditional setting and the contemporary choices in the plantings." She and the clients agreed on a quiet palette of colors—combinations of lavender, pale green, and white, along with a variety of tall grasses and plantings that would sway with the winds. "The garden has a lot of movement," Jordin emphasizes.

Beneath the surface of the house, though, are more design surprises. Durkin proposed that the interior walls and ceilings be clad with seven-inch-wide oak boards, wire-brushed to reveal texture. The most conspicuous interior design detail, the boards run on the horizontal throughout the first level but shift to the vertical on the second. In a sense, the house is turned inside out. Once the rhythm and dimension of the boards were agreed upon by both the architects and interior designer, the agenda for the interiors proceeded apace. Durkin likens the interior clapboarding to a "casualizing" of a house that also manages formality, certainly in its proportions and detailing. "We all chose a regionally appropriate set of design elements," Durkin emphasizes, "with the boarding, something of a surprise, being one of them." These and other design solutions from Durkin often result from his penchant for drawing, his favorite medium for communicating with architects and clients. Team meetings with Durkin, the architects, and often the clients together around a conference table required multiple rolls of tracing paper as design ideas and solutions were sketched into reality.

In keeping with Ferguson & Shamamian's declaration that when one enters a house one leaves behind all expectations based on the exterior, there is the stair hall. An entire room, situated within its own gabled expanse, solely contains a sinuous, sculptural floating staircase. The room, evocative of a Quaker meetinghouse in its purity, scale, and hue, is a sanctuary for artwork, part of a notable collection to which the homeowners continue to add. One could easily conclude that the stairway itself is a work of minimalist art; its shape has been likened to a corkscrew, a spiral, an unfurled

ribbon, a sculpture. As a work of engineering, it's not a simple spiral staircase that continues to turn in the same direction, thereby supporting itself. Rather, it takes an unexpected turn in the opposite direction at the top, which is achieved by utilizing structural support from all of the stair's elements, including treads, risers, and even the handrail and pickets, which act as a truss. Although engaging artworks fill the interiors, the stairway stands out as, perhaps, the largest design element one experiences upon entering the room. Here is proof that a functional, structural element, when articulated properly, elevates to become a work of art.

As for the shade of white that coats the boards—what appears to be a simple milk wash—Durkin estimates that he and his team tried fifty versions. "White" is merely a catch-all word for the nearly infinite versions of the shade. The challenge to painting the interior of a home on Nantucket is to allow for the often gray cast that shrouds the island. There is, of course, the great colorizer, the Atlantic Ocean, coupled with the northerly location of the island. On clear, sunny days, a white that is too bright would result in a cacophony of interior reflections. Yellows need to be avoided since the color assumes a somber, peaked cast on cloudy days. Durkin and the clients settled on a white infused with a touch of taupe. The outside trim, however, is a pure white, a color approved by the HDC.

This is the third home Ferguson & Shamamian has designed for the clients, and the latest of several for which Durkin has done the interior design. The wife is known for being a visionary collaborator, someone who is able to help all the parties establish authenticity, style, and quality in

Previous spread, left: Not wishing to detract
from the sculptural stair, the owners limited art
here to photographs by Wolfgang Tillmans in
different sizes and, as the artist himself often does,
hung them casually, some framed and some on
clips. The "light string" at the stair's center is by
Félix González-Torres. *Previous spread, right*: The
determined alignment of the interior boards, with
no disruptions from door to jambs to inside jambs,
continues uninterrupted throughout the interiors.

Left: A patiently awaited gouache by George
Condo hangs in the living room; the library is visible
through the open doorway.

Following spread, left: The breakfast room. *Following
spread, right*: A private stairway leads to the beach.

her homes. Because both the architects and Durkin have
worked with her and her husband for more than twenty
years, the two design teams understand and respect her
aesthetic. Members of the Ferguson & Shamamian team
speak fondly of how thoughtfully and energetically she
responds to plans and drawings they present. She is able
to balance the artistry of a house with its functionality.
Durkin emphasizes that one of the most satisfying aspects of
their collaboration is her talent for foreseeing the results
and enjoying the design in its built form. Apart from her
occasional repositioning of artworks, the client rarely
changes design elements once they are in place.

As for the art on the walls, that alone is one of the
great narrative plotlines of the house. Durkin emphasizes
that while he is not involved in the selection of art or the
arrangement of the pieces, or even privy to the clients'
buying of new works, he is responsible for designing interiors that can adapt to any work of art that might arrive.
He knows his job as an interior designer is successful
when he furnishes a room in such a way that the space can
receive any new artwork.

The clients commissioned conceptual artist Lawrence
Weiner, noted for his text-centric paintings, for a site-
specific work on the back wall of the pool house. Ferguson &
Shamamian consulted with the artist about his requirements
for wall surface and preparation. Weiner matter-of-factly
responded that what he needed was "just a wall for words."
He painted:

> Delineated overlapping lines
> marked by the glint of the sun
> on the foam left behind
> from the movement of the tide

While the sentiment is an unresolved sentence fragment,
it does speak to much of the design process for the finished
house. Designers, architects, and clients came together
to create something that is safely secured onshore, protected
from the tide, and that when seen in "the glint of the
sun" stands out in its setting. The house is that rare, perfect
whelk discovered on the beach.

Above, clockwise from top left: A flair detail resolves the shingles at the door jamb; the front porch; a children's bunkroom.
Opposite, clockwise from top left: A guest bedroom beneath a valley rafter; the dining room and living room beyond; the rear porch.

Following spread: An evening view of the pool house with a stenciled text sculpture by conceptual artist Lawrence Weiner.
The Ugo Rondinone sculpture is a cast of a 2,000-year-old olive tree placed so the owners can view it from the kitchen and family room.

THE PARTY GOES ON

A prominent New York couple renovates
an apartment that played a starring role
in the city's social life. The rooms are now filled
with new guests and family.

Previous spread, left and right: In the apartment's entry and gallery, a floor pattern conceived by interior designer Jacques Grange echoes the original ceiling tracery. A bright, contemporary, pearl-white faux bois painted by Uriu Nuance covers what was once dark oak paneling.

———

Right: Old space, new use—the entrance gallery has been transformed into a room for entertaining. *Below*: At home, the apartment's former owner, socialite Anne Slater.

ertain New York City apartments come with provenance. And maybe even some (friendly) ghosts. Years ago, before the new owners of this second-floor apartment on Fifth Avenue moved in, the previous resident, the socialite Anne Slater, used to open her Tudor-Jacobean–motif door to the likes of Hollywood (and actual) royalty—Grace Kelly, Fred Astaire, Bing Crosby (who slept and practiced dance steps in a back bedroom), and the Duke and Duchess of Windsor. Slater was herself a queen of New York social life in the 1960s, '70s, and '80s, and while the parties she hosted in the apartment have long since ended, the new owners are well aware of those spirited fêtes.

Left: The living room walls are finished in marmorino plaster, noted
for its ability to take on a variety of hues and painted textures.
Above: Grange responded to the clients' desire for their son to be able
to play ping-pong in the living room on a Ron Arad table.

Right: The grains and hues of palm-wood panels from Atelier Viollet and custom hardware from H. Theophile combine to form a door separating the living and dining rooms.

Following spread, left: From a window with mirrored jambs, views of the Metropolitan Museum of Art.
Following spread, right: In this dressing room niche, Grange recreated the rough cerusing that was a favored technique of Jean-Michel Frank.

Although the couple wanted to make the spacious apartment very much their own, and fill it with guests and contemporary artwork, they respected the party provenance of their new home and liked the idea of honoring its past. Unlike Slater, neither the husband nor the wife sports trademark cobalt-blue eyeglasses, but they do welcome visitors into a home dramatically changed, updated, contemporized, and bright. Slater might not recognize some of the redone rooms and their new roles, but as a connoisseur herself, she would recognize the quality of the altered layout and decor.

Upon first meeting with the clients, Ferguson & Shamamian became immediately aware of the couple's deep knowledge of design, particularly mid- to late twentieth-century modern furniture and decorative arts. In fact, for that first meeting, they showed up with seven mood boards, each a kind of timeline of modern design. They agreed to eliminate an oval reception room in favor of a single large living room melded with a dining room; add a spacious island in the kitchen; reconfigure the back-of-the-house staff quarters; and turn the gallery into a dedicated reception area and sitting room. Early on, too, they set out to find the right interior designer, a search they undertook with the same zeal with which they purchase contemporary art. They wanted someone already at the top of his or her profession, who through collaboration could also enrich and expand their understanding of design.

Jacques Grange, *un grand homme* of interior design, was commissioned to transform the interiors. The Paris-based Grange recalls the couple's passion for design and enthusiasm for working in consort with him during the nearly two-year-long process. Grange says that the wife even offered, half-jokingly, to come to Paris to work in his office as an assistant. Instead, Grange encouraged her to go to design school, while he emphasized that she already had mastered some of the material she'd likely encounter in coursework.

This 1912 building, designed by McKim, Mead & White architects and situated across the street from the

Metropolitan Museum of Art, was one of the early apartment buildings in New York that architects conceived of as a new alternative for luxe urban residential life (which, for the wealthy, had previously existed only in townhouses and mansions). Luxury apartment buildings were not yet common in America. Certain early apartment buildings of that era, this among the best examples, incorporated Tudor and Jacobean architectural details, motifs then popular in select upscale townhouse interiors and suburban residences. It was thought that if apartment buildings incorporated such details—coffered ceilings, tracery, paneling, quatrefoils, limestone floors—society people would be drawn to the multiple-family dwellings. In fact, every apartment on every floor of this building includes the same details. Apart from the Tudor and Jacobean references, the living rooms and dining rooms are typically Georgian in style, the salons Adamesque. Early twentieth-century luxury Manhattan apartments needed to embrace European style roots in order to attract a certain American clientele.

Ferguson & Shamamian, the clients, and Grange concurred that certain extant details should remain. Instead of history being completely erased, it was to be acknowledged and celebrated, while at the same time revitalized for today. In what was the apartment's gallery, elaborate original tracery and paneling define the ceilings and walls. Grange and the architects enlivened those surfaces by painting them white, then graining them in faux bois to return the look of wood to them, but then Grange did something even bolder. He echoed that tracery by designing an abstract zigzagging pattern for the floor that artisans realized in black and white tiles. He achieved the same effect in other rooms, notably in a guest bath with a flooring pattern that references a Roberto Burle Marx design found on Rio de Janeiro sidewalks, and elsewhere in the apartment with especially vigorous chevron flooring.

For the main bath, Grange guided the couple toward silver travertine surfaces, perhaps an homage to Jean-Michel Frank, whose bathrooms he admired. Early on, Grange handed Ferguson & Shamamian a rough sketch of what he envisioned for the room. It was up to the architects to fashion slim but sturdy metal armatures inset with ultrathin slabs of marble, an example of a minimalist detail that requires considerable contemporary engineering.

As for that entry gallery, originally more of a transitional space than one for lingering, it has since morphed into an actual room, with defined seating

areas, oversized art, sculptural furniture, and a bar set with stools, the latter indicating its new role as an entertaining space. In fact, given the flexibility of the now-opened living and dining rooms, which, in turn, open to the kitchen, the owners may entertain in a variety of ways and on different scales. The owners also did something rather brave in the room—covering an existing window, albeit one with an interior courtyard view, in order to create more wall space for artwork.

Ferguson & Shamamian responded accordingly in the kitchen, visually brightening a once dark room with a faux skylight that hovers over the new kitchen island. So convincing are the panes of glass above, a contemporary interpretation of Tudoresque tracery, that visitors standing there might think they are looking up and out to the sky. The kitchen is now a large, open room for entertaining, not an uncommon dynamic today in both apartments and houses.

In response to the owners' request, Ferguson & Shamamian had originally conceived of the child's bath as featuring a living aquarium, in deference to the son's passion for fish. But that idea quickly proved problematic, for few co-op boards would be keen to have 2,000 gallons of water sloshing around directly above their grand lobbies, and this one was no exception. As a compromise, the firm found Italian tiles depicting oversized fish and crustaceans, schools of which now swim along the walls, into and out of the shower. The child has other venues for play in the apartment, including a Ron Arad–designed stainless-steel ping-pong table set up in the living room overlooking Fifth Avenue. Such is the tenor of the clients, who are decidedly contemporary, not only in their art collecting habits, but also in how they live day to day. The ghost of Anne Slater might eye that playing surface as a spot for canapés when the bespoke table is not in use for a game. (No doubt the table would have suited the hostess who once invited a dancing bear from the circus to one of her parties.)

The finished project represented not only a collaboration among the parties, but also a dialogue with the past. The apartment was once occupied by a vibrant personality and her friends, and its architecture embodied historical precedents, some of which were featured on the clients' mood boards. While the apartment's old history has been re-established, a new history has also begun.

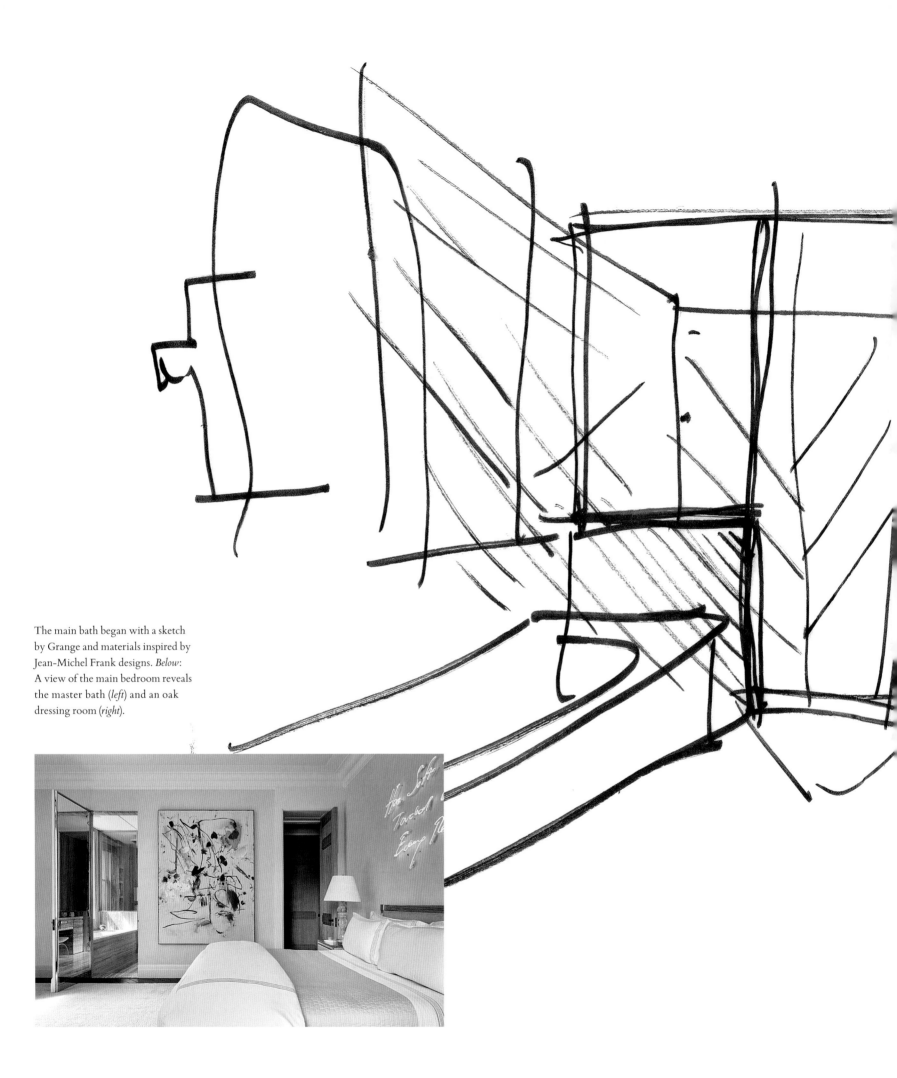

The main bath began with a sketch by Grange and materials inspired by Jean-Michel Frank designs. *Below*: A view of the main bedroom reveals the master bath (*left*) and an oak dressing room (*right*).

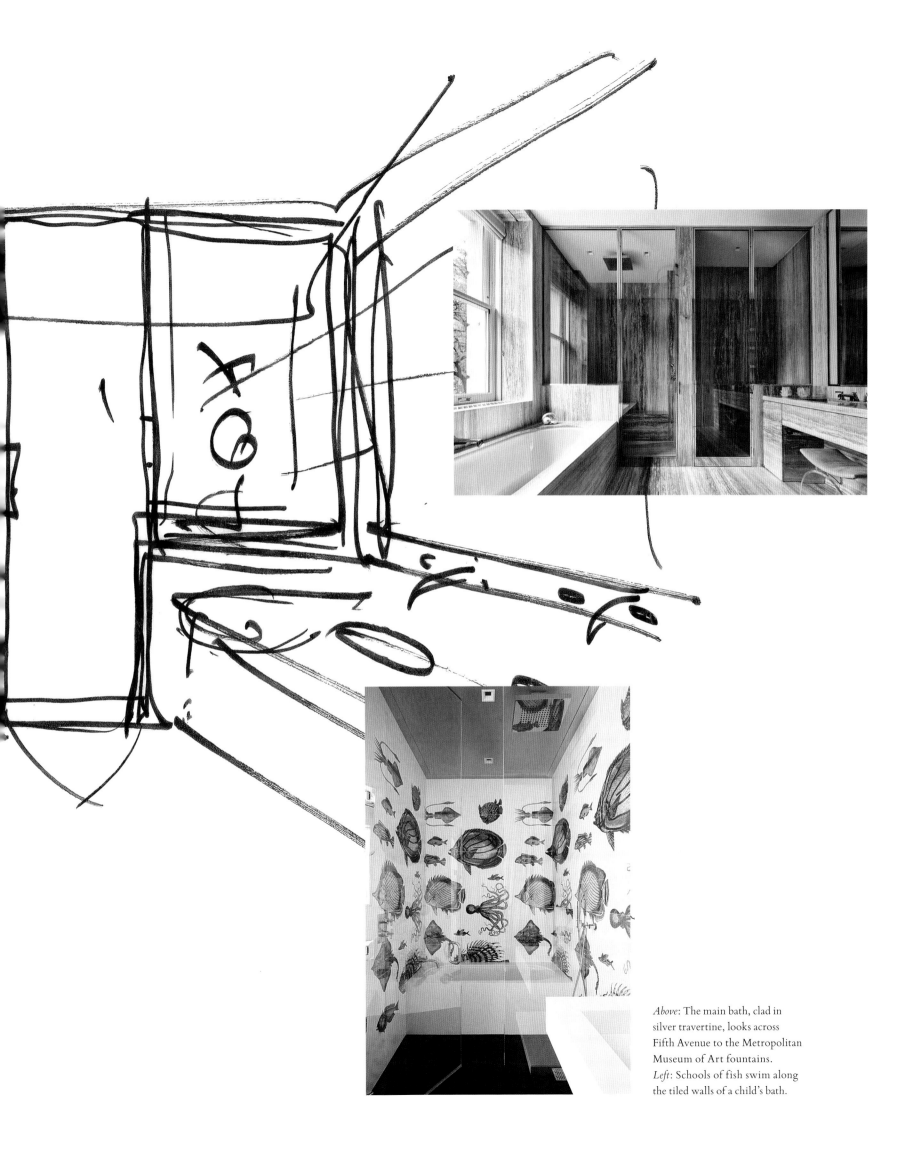

Above: The main bath, clad in silver travertine, looks across Fifth Avenue to the Metropolitan Museum of Art fountains.
Left: Schools of fish swim along the tiled walls of a child's bath.

TAKING PLACE

A couple wanted their home on Florida's Intracoastal Waterway
to fit seamlessly into their lives, into the community, and onto
the land itself. They relied on their instincts and the talents of the
design team to achieve that.

Previous spread, left: A coral outcropping was discovered during excavation and was carved into a retaining wall by SMI Landscape Architecture. *Previous spread, right*: A glimpse of the Intracoastal from the main bedroom balcony.

Opposite: The ground floor loggia adjacent to the dining and living rooms culminates in a lush canopy of trees outside of the library. *Left*: A watercolor study of the front elevation.

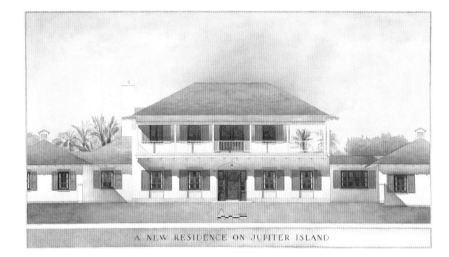

A NEW RESIDENCE ON JUPITER ISLAND

*i*n order to build a sound house, two things are essential: trust and patience. Clients must trust their own instincts, as well as the talents of their architect, interior designer, landscape architect, and contractor . . . and all must accept that waiting can yield the best results. Before embarking on the design of a new house on Florida's Jupiter Island, these homeowners made the firm decision to engage a team they had worked with previously and made a commitment to patience during the process.

The clients entrusted their longtime interior designer, Victoria Hagan, to envision the rooms in their new Anglo-Caribbean–style house. Upon first beginning her work in concert with Ferguson & Shamamian, with which she has enjoyed a decades-long and fruitful affiliation, Hagan recalls, "This whole project began with trust, as well as a mutual respect. This Florida house represented the culmination of all the qualities and characteristics that brought our work to the next level."

The strong, amiable, collaborative atmosphere also proved a challenge, but each participant—homeowners, architects, designer—was determined to answer fully the needs of the others. "Each party was looking at a different aspect of the house," says the wife, "but we went through the process in harmony. The minute Oscar Shamamian puts pen to paper, you're included—and off you go."

One of the most admirable—and applicable—traits of the homeowners is their talent for research. The husband is at the top of his field for good reason, and he approached this house in the same way that he pursues everything in life—through careful research, questioning, and the pursuit of the highest standards of excellence. Part of the process for the home-owners involved their patience and willingness to pause.

Long before the couple moved into the finished house, they had spent time, in a sense, living in it, occupying rooms that didn't yet exist. Before the design was finalized, they lived for more than a year in an extant house on the site, learning the land so they would know exactly where to situate the new house and gain a sense of how they would occupy it once completed. Well in advance of construction, they were familiar with how sunlight shines on the property at different times of day, the effects of breezes off the water, even the sounds of the advancing and ebbing tides at the shoreline of their land. They resolved which views they wanted, and those they wished to obscure. "We took our time," the husband says, "and that proved to be an important piece of the building process. Once we learned what we wanted, we knocked the old house down and began the new."

During their waiting game, the couple learned, for instance, that they needed to shift the position of the house by some fifteen feet to maximize views. The owner took it upon himself to research every detail and educate himself so he understood the process required to obtain the proper variances. As a result, his presentation to the town board to build a new house on the property was a success, and Oscar Shamamian characterizes it as "the most sincere and articulate plea I've ever heard from a client."

While the design for the house originated with what is now referred to by all as "scheme A," it wasn't until they had reached "scheme U" that the final design was realized. Scheme U is certainly a subset of A, and every drawing in between reflected change, increased refinement, and greater collective understanding by all. Nuances matter. The hand-drawn ideas expressed on those pieces of paper range from houses with formal symmetrical layouts to those with more open-ended plans. Some versions reveal dwellings with one story, others two. Some designs evoke residences compact in scale, while others are more rambling. In retrospect, the twenty-one schemes had much in common: a central mass containing the main rooms, flanked by wings for the kitchen, family rooms, and bedrooms.

Right: The front elevation reveals the precise symmetry of the Anglo-Caribbean–style house—a five-bay composition topped by a hip roof, with one-story wings positioned on either side. *Below*: The fifth bay of the main block is deliberately omitted to allow for the main bedroom porch.

Oscar Shamamian describes the careful design process as having been "fun and scary," because the clients "tested themselves and they tested us in all the right ways." The plans evolved as the clients learned more about what they wanted, and everyone adapted and remained, literally, on the same page.

The couple admires Ferguson & Shamamian for the firm's ability to capture historical precedents and honor vernacular forms—in this case, the house is inspired by the colonial architecture of St. Augustine, Florida, and the Anglo-Caribbean style. The homeowners embraced the forms that the architects had devised—a residence with broad verandas; expansive porches; a hip roof with deep, sweeping overhangs; bottom-paneled French doors framed by full-length shutters; and five-bay symmetry. The approved Anglo-Caribbean precedent was modified by incorporating an open-ended bay in the composition, a non-canonical solution. This provided for a shaded, covered porch as part of the second-floor main suite, a request from the clients. Visible upon arrival, single-story wings extend forward to embrace the land. On the northernmost border, a discreet guesthouse appears as yet another wing. Exterior spaces—sunny open-air terraces and decks, shaded porches—become additional rooms.

The most visceral experience of this house occurs at its center-placed entrance. From there, a visitor immediately sees through the house to the waterway. That first impression reveals a house both formal and not, private and open, expansive and modest. At the rear of the house, which faces the Intracoastal, a hypnotic, even heroic, rhythm of white square piers runs along the full length of the first-floor porch.

Previous spread: The major rooms of the house are aligned enfilade, with a colonnaded screen running
the full length, allowing for a floorplan that is both open and formal.

Opposite: The kitchen and breakfast room with a wall of ganged windows and doors and an
open-trussed ceiling. *Above*: View of the living room with the study beyond.

127

Above: The relatively simple character of this house is offset by the variety and richness of ceiling treatments—some of which are flat with boards while others display tray ceilings in various forms. *Opposite*: An ancient ficus tree flourishes near the guesthouse.

Inside, the rooms flow in an enfilade, the term for a layout in which all rooms are linked directly, rather than via corridors. The enfilade arrangement fosters natural cross-lighting (since there are windows on opposite sides of the room) and captures long, through views that encourage togetherness. Yet privacy is easily gained, especially in this house, simply by stepping farther into a room, out of sight.

More by accident than by intention, every room appears to focus on a single work of art. While the couple continue to add to their collection of contemporary art, they insist nothing was bought specifically for this house. "First and foremost, we wanted a home that was easy to live in," says the wife, "definitely not an art house." They shipped existing artworks from their other homes. Once the pieces arrived, Hagan, with her deep understanding of the clients and her uncanny sense for where everything should be placed, intuited the perfect spot for each piece.

Through extensive research, the clients gained a great deal of knowledge about the region's flora and chose landscape architect Jorge Sánchez to create the right effect. "The clients wanted the old Hobe Sound look—natural, lush, and windswept," says Sánchez, who eschews the area's trend of clipped hedges and formal gardens. The effect was achieved through a dense perimeter of multilayered and varied plantings, as well as lawns dotted with palms and large, old, relocated ficus trees. Sánchez recalls being pleasantly charged and challenged by the substantial elevation change at the rear of the property—almost twenty-five feet from the house to the water's edge— which enabled the creation of three graded terraces culminating in Venetian steps down to the beach. The excavation for the pool revealed that the property sits on a natural coral ledge. Sánchez took advantage of this fortuitous discovery by exposing the ridge between the pool terrace and the lower lawn as a retaining wall. As they dug out the pool, large pieces of coral were salvaged and placed at the water's edge as a natural seawall. So naturally does the house sit in its landscape that it appears to have been there for generations.

Looking back, Oscar Shamamian recalls, "The clients pushed us to answer every hope they had for their house, and we continued on, trusting we were all working toward the same goal." With the house long completed, the achievements are renewed daily as if the goals were brand-new. "Something special happens every time I walk inside," says the wife. "Each time I get to experience the house all over again."

131

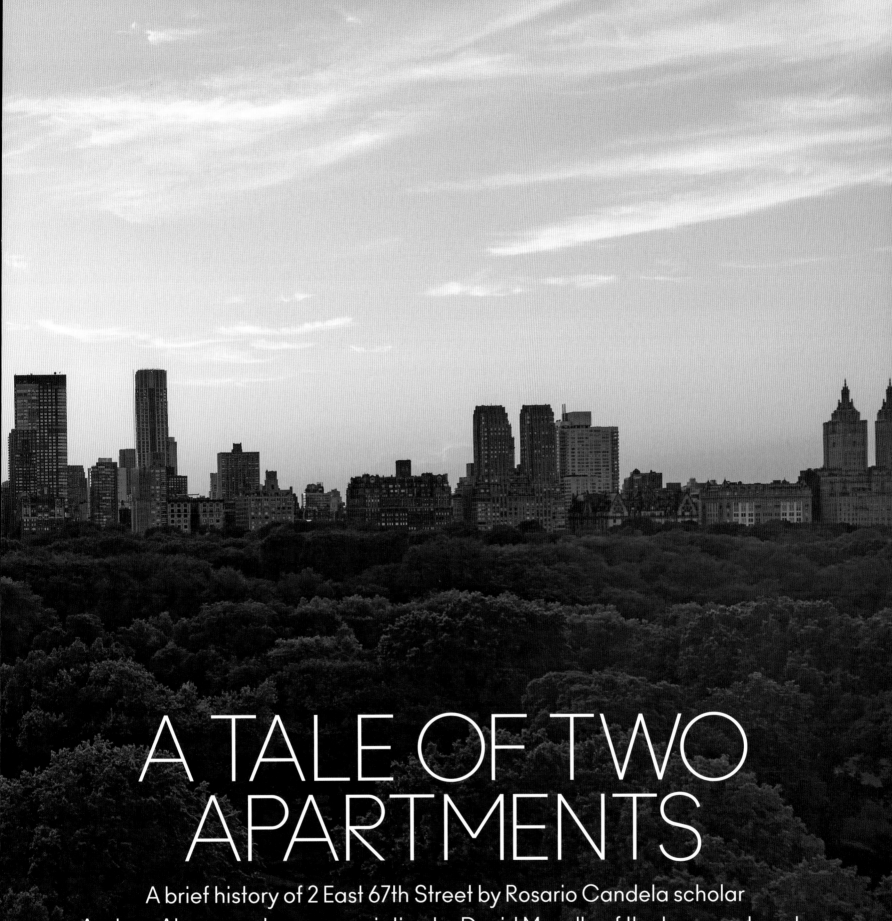

A TALE OF TWO APARTMENTS

A brief history of 2 East 67th Street by Rosario Candela scholar
Andrew Alpern and an appreciation by David Masello of the two apartments
transformed by Ferguson & Shamamian in the venerable building.

A FIFTH AVENUE ADDRESS is so highly coveted that developers have been known to finagle one for buildings that are one hundred feet away from the avenue. Yet this elegant, fully limestone-clad building actually on the avenue is modestly known as 2 East 67th Street. There's a battle story behind that address. During the late nineteenth and early twentieth centuries, magnificent mansions were erected on Fifth Avenue, many of which took side-street addresses in order to project an air of quiet self-assurance that helped to separate the knowledgeable from the newcomer. But not everyone was so modestly low-key, and when a corner house took a Fifth Avenue address, in some cases the adjoining house on the side street called itself number 1 or number 2 East. Stuart Duncan did that at East 75th Street, even though his lot was, in fact, at number 3. When Edward Harkness replaced the old corner building with a spiffy new mansion in 1908 (still there), he styled his address as 1 East 75th Street, forcing Duncan to yield the coveted numero uno.

Judge Elbert H. Gary lived in a house on the south corner of 66th Street that looked remarkably like the one Edward Harkness built, and that carried the address of 856 Fifth Avenue. Former governor Nathan Miller lived next door and felt secure taking the address of 2 East 67th Street. When Judge Gary's widow sold her former home to Michael E. Paterno (she would buy an apartment in the building he erected on the site), the developer opted for a decidedly low-key approach for his new project. High on the list was using the side-street address to which the lot was entitled. Miller didn't want to give up his address, however, so initially Paterno called his building 856 Fifth Avenue. But he also called in his lawyers to claim his right to the 2 East 67th Street address. The building was completed late in 1928, but it wasn't until 1930 that the right of the building to have the side-street address was established. Curiously, the initial residents used the Fifth Avenue address, with the side street one taking twenty years to be fully adopted.

In keeping with its low-key address, architect Rosario Candela (1890–1953) and the associated firm of Warren & Wetmore designed the new apartment house with a far more quiet hand than was customary for them. Everything about the façade is restrained almost to the point of total silence. While the lower three floors are conventionally rusticated, the belt-course frieze immediately above is completely plain. And the rest of the façade all the way up to the two vestigial cornices is totally unadorned planar slabs of flawless limestone. There aren't even any accentuating moldings around the windows, except at the top floor, which also boasts some arches. This is a building that speaks at the level of Marcel Marceau.

At this remove in time, and with no extant office files to reveal their secrets, there is no way of knowing who was responsible for what. But high-profile personalities might suggest a backstory. The Italian immigrant Rosario Candela brought with him from Palermo an instinctive feel for sculptural carving and delicate ornament, which is evident in his other work. Warren & Wetmore's aesthetic was bolder and at times quite aggressive. So the brief for the appearance of 2 East 67th Street has to have originated with Michael Paterno. The youngest of the prolific apartment house–building extended family of the Paterno brothers and their in-laws, the Campagnas, Michael was perhaps the most imaginative of them all, responsive to changing times and open to new ideas. Perhaps he had been influenced by Dorothy Draper (1889–1969), or perhaps he felt that a quieter building would stand out in what was at the time a very crowded market of haute-luxe apartment buildings. The reasoning behind its design may be elusive, but the building itself remains to impress and give pleasure both to its residents and to passersby.

—*ANDREW ALPERN*

A COMMON GOAL, if not fantasy, of New York apartment dwellers is to see their neighbors' apartments. Although layouts are often identical, especially along the same line, the moment one enters another apartment, the mood, light, views, and decor all seem different. Such is the effect at 2 East 67th Street, with these two full-floor apartments that Ferguson & Shamamian renovated and, indeed, transformed.

The experience of a home, especially in an apartment building, begins not just at the front door but with its materials, form, and surface design. A statement at the vestibule already distinguishes your apartment from your neighbor's. But 2 East 67th Street, a twelve-story, limestone-clad edifice completed in 1928 by Rosario Candela, is no common building. So spacious and luxurious are the full-floor units by the era's master residential-building architect, credited with designing eighty-one apartment houses in New York, that each assumes the feel and scale of a house. Yet every apartment on every floor of the building has an identical layout, with an area hovering around 5,300 square feet. Go high enough in the building and the treetops are cleared, allowing for that much-coveted view over Central Park. With apartments, views alone become a central feature of decor; what is seen outside the windows helps determine the mood and atmosphere inside.

For the two projects Ferguson & Shamamian was commissioned to renovate in the building—one comprising the eighth floor, the other the eleventh floor—the resulting layouts, even after the gutting and re-erecting of walls, remained largely faithful to the original plan. In both residences, the public rooms still face west over the park, bedrooms are configured along the north spine, and a mix of dressing rooms and studies/offices are situated on the south side. The original floorplans proved so sound that it made little sense to alter them in any significant manner. Staff quarters, once de rigueur in such buildings, are often the first spaces to be reconfigured, and that was done in each of these apartments. These layouts adhere to a directive Candela once conveyed to students at New York's Beaux-Arts Institute of Design: "An apartment, excepting a one-room unit, is composed of two well defined sections... the living quarters and the sleeping quarters, and in the case of luxurious apartments, a third one, the service quarters."

Why is each finished apartment such a distinctive home if so much has remained the same? One could point to the artworks on display, the windows, and the decor, each carried out by namesake interior design firms. As for that front door, the residence on floor eight features a see-through glass entry, so that the moment one exits the elevator, a view through the apartment to Central Park and beyond to the West Side comes into focus. In the other apartment, an imposing pair of handsome burnished nickel doors, defined by a Greek key–like pattern, greets visitors from the elevator. The finishes, moldings, and architectural detailing by Ferguson & Shamamian are other defining moments, which is semi-ironic, in that the exterior of 2 East 67th Street is conspicuously constrained.

It's not often that an architecture firm has the opportunity to work this thoroughly on two apartments in the same building. While this is not the kind of building in which neighbors typically knock on one another's door asking to borrow cups of sugar, the residents do share a common sensibility and sensitivity to design. To live in a Candela creation is a privilege. Despite the worldly success of the building's residents, each of these clients would likely be intrigued by the other's home, and perhaps even flattered, as it is ultimately a part of theirs, too.

—DAVID MASELLO

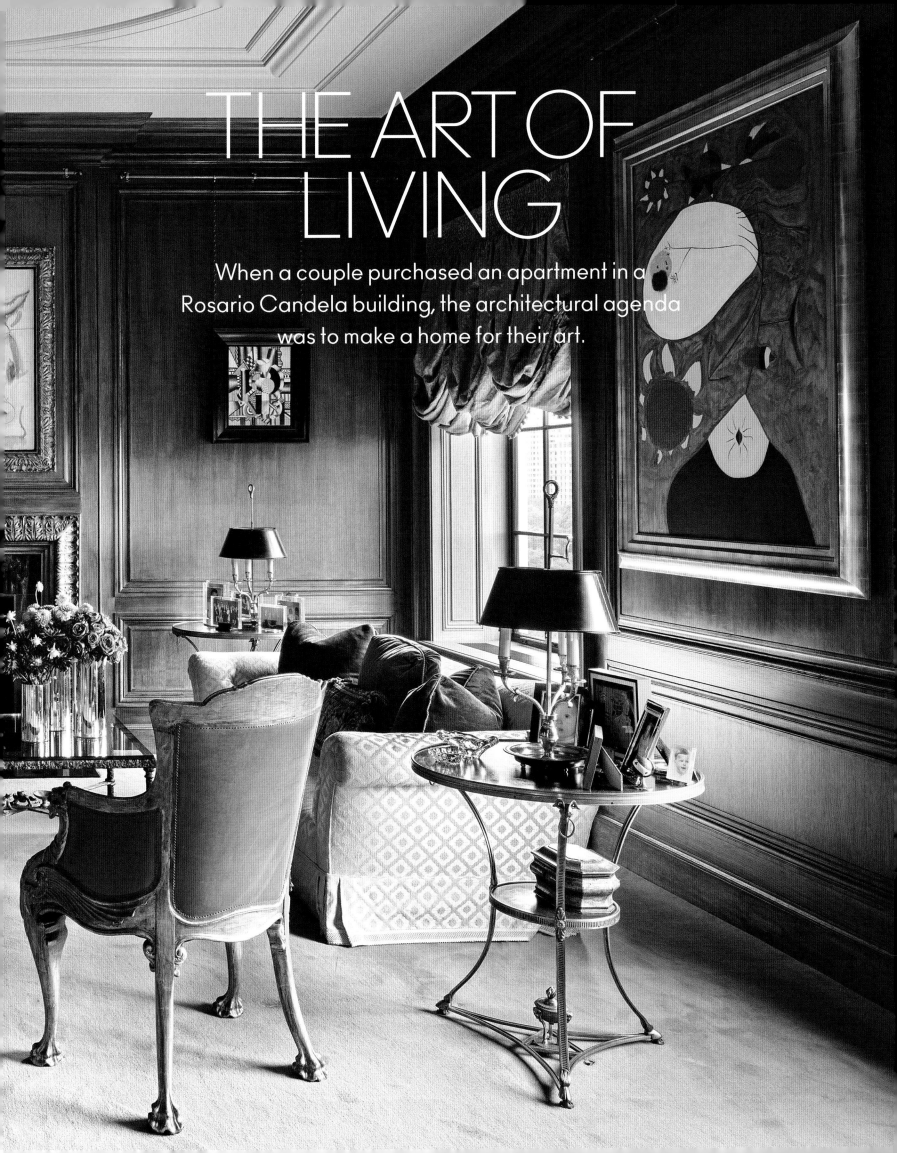

THE ART OF LIVING

When a couple purchased an apartment in a Rosario Candela building, the architectural agenda was to make a home for their art.

*U*nlike most full-floor apartments on Fifth Avenue, this one begins with a big surprise. The moment the elevator door opens, a visitor sees not only across the whole of Central Park but also, front and center, Joan Miró's *Portrait IV*. Such visual choreography was intentional.

The homeowner, one of the most influential figures in the art museum world, wanted the front door to be both secure, of course, *and* transparent. Instead of the typical entry experience of a solid door in a windowless vestibule, she wanted guests, upon arrival, to look into—and through—the apartment, giving them insight into who she is as a person and as a patron of the arts. To achieve such transparency requires the right materials and the right frame of mind. The homeowner and her (now late) husband collected important art for decades—Léger, Kandinsky, Pollock, Miró, Dubuffet— displaying the works, loaning them, curating them. So open is she to sharing what she and her husband collected that she wishes to reveal much of it right at the threshold. As a pivotal leader of the arts and the museum world, she is dedicated to making great works of art available to the public. This apartment may be her private domain, but she wishes to maintain a sense of public access to the art she owns.

She had Ferguson & Shamamian design a front door made of lightweight steel, brass, and tempered glass. It took some twenty sketched-out versions before the right design, based loosely on a nineteenth-century door found in a French ironworks catalogue, was agreed upon. Because the homeowner has such a fine eye for art and design, she had initially envisioned her apartment door echoing, in appearance, the front door to the building itself. That building is a notable 1928 structure by Rosario Candela, whose lobby the Parish-Hadley interior design firm had been commissioned to redecorate in the 1980s, a period when Mark Ferguson and Oscar Shamamian were staff architects.

Similar to another apartment in the same building that Ferguson & Shamamian later redesigned, this one, too, was gutted, with the original layout largely replicated. The owners, architects, and interior designers from Parish-Hadley concurred that the bones of this Candela building were so sound that it made no sense to alter the anatomy. However, a series of dark, cramped back-of-the-house staff quarters, an area the homeowner recalls as having been so claustrophobic that upon visiting the apartment as a prospective buyer she wanted to flee, was transformed into a large study, dressing room, and bath for her husband. Given the layout changes that

Pages 140–141: The dining room has an elaborate marquetry floor and a heavily articulated ceiling, while the walls were left unadorned to allow the art, including Roy Lichtenstein's *Girl with Piano* and Ellsworth Kelly's *Bay*, to stand out.

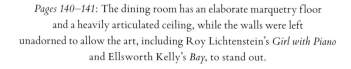

Previous spread, left: An antique wooden curtain detail. *Previous spread, right*: Alberto Giacometti's *Le Nez*.

Above and opposite: To avoid the kinds of hallways Oscar Shamamian describes as "long run-on sentences," the bedroom hall is punctuated with a six-and-a-half-foot-diameter dome at its center, below which hangs Francis Bacon's *Crouching Nude*.

Left: The east wall of the dining room pairs sculptural and visual works. *Below*: Fernand Léger's *The Luncheon* in the library.

were made, the homeowner speaks of having created a more expansive home with fewer rooms.

The homeowners raised their two children in what she now refers to as a "real family" apartment on Park Avenue. But after the children had grown up, she and her husband purchased this apartment, citing it as a "more adult space"—that is, one in which their artworks could be displayed to full effect. She was prepared to do whatever it took to achieve that goal, stating, in fact, that this undertaking did not represent her "first rodeo," a reference to prior and current residences, some of which were designed by Ferguson & Shamamian and Parish-Hadley.

The architectural agenda for this transformation was about the art and its makers. Those artists, some alive, some deceased, were active participants, in a sense, in the decision-making. Although the homeowner knew where she wanted the canvases and sculptures to be placed, it was up to Ferguson & Shamamian and the interior designers to create the right backdrop. The architects responded with novel designs for decorative ceilings and cornices, with some rooms demarcated by black marble baseboards for a frame-like effect. But the walls throughout were left smooth, uninterrupted and unembellished by chair rails or paneling. The interior designers, meanwhile, used few curtains in order to preserve expanses of wall.

One notable exception regarding window treatments, however, was in the formal dining room. Brian Murphy, an associate at Parish-Hadley at the time, had long coveted a set of carved, wooden curtains made in France in the mid-nineteenth century that he found in a 57th Street antiques shop. He went with the client to see the objects; she was taken by their quirky sculptural quality and asked that they be placed in the dining room. With their faux tiebacks, deep pleats, and sinuous ruffles, the curtains were cut to fit the windows and now are permanently drawn to reveal park and street views.

Another architecturally defining feature of Ferguson & Shamamian's work is a spacious central hallway that functions as a gallery for art. The homeowner was adamant that she did not want one of the windowless four-foot-wide internal hallways that typically link public and private

rooms in apartments found in prewar buildings of this caliber. Rather, she envisioned a hallway expansive enough that it allowed the art to be viewed from a perspective that could never be accommodated by a narrow space.

The resulting six-and-a-half-foot-wide corridor is accentuated at its center with a dome, supported by fluted pilasters with Tower of the Winds capitals. The dome is so alluring and surprising that one can't help but pause to look up into it, expecting to find a clerestory cupola or a painted scene within. Instead, ambient lighting fills the shell. This hallway space is defined by Francis Bacon's emerald green *Crouching Nude,* in front of which Murphy positioned a low bench. While the idea of someone sitting there and leaning back into the canvas may be a concern, Oscar Shamamian speaks of a summer he spent during college working as a gallery guard in the Museum of Modern Art, an experience that taught him how a strategically placed bench in front of a painting acts more as a barrier than as a welcoming seating area.

While the artworks are by some of the most important names of the twentieth century, artistic moments appear as well in more ancillary spaces, such as a powder room. The walls of a half bath are adorned with scenes from a lacquered eighteenth-century Chinese Coromandel screen purchased at a Christie's sale of items from the estate of Marietta Tree. However, when Parish-Hadley undertook the task of having the screen cut into panels to cover the walls, it was discovered that there weren't enough panels to fill the surface. An artisan replicated the detailed scenes on new panels, with the resulting work so seamless that the difference between the original and the recreated is imperceptible.

Because the client was so sure about what she wanted and because Ferguson & Shamamian and the Parish-Hadley team knew how to respond to her directives, the apartment has remained virtually unchanged since it was completed in 2000. The homeowner never tires of her art, nor of the views she sees out to the park. Of the place she occupies, the homeowner says, "I'm high enough to have views, but low enough to see people on the street. It's very nice to be able to have that human contact while in my home."

Above, clockwise from top left: A view from the study, which incorporates faux tortoiseshell trim, into the main bedroom; a butler's room was opened to the dining room to create a breakfast nook; Chinese Coromandel screens (and seamlessly integrated replicas) fill the walls of a powder room; the main bedroom. *Opposite*: Behind a mahogany door from the main bedroom, the tub is fashioned of green onyx with sterling silver hardware from P. E. Guerin; the carvings on the tub front reference a traditional French design.

PERSONALITY DRIVEN

This influential couple allowed their apartment building to have a strong voice in the design of their home.

Previous spread: A Lobmeyr crystal starburst chandelier illuminates glass cast moldings and mica wall treatment in the dining room.

Opposite: Nickel and lacquer doors by Mead & Josipovich, evocative of 1930s reductivist Classicism, mark the entrance from the elevator vestibule. *Below*: In the kitchen, the walls and backsplash are fashioned of blue glass tiles.

Some buildings start with big egos—not necessarily those of their residents, but those of their developers. This is particularly true of Manhattan apartment buildings designed by the prolific and revered Rosario Candela built in the 1920s and '30s. Those who commissioned Candela were seeking to attract a clientele of a certain caliber, and the resulting buildings brought prestige to their respective neighborhoods.

This 1928 structure comes imbued not only with the architectural pedigree of Candela, but also that of Dorothy Draper, the visionary interior designer of her day, famous for her embrace not only of bold stripes but also of classical detailing. Candela consulted Draper during the planning of this project to ensure that every aspect of the twelve-story building would be an exemplar of the Georgian Revival style inside, though with reductivist neoclassical exterior façades. Candela likely knew that Draper's involvement in the building would enhance its profile and place it in the fashionable spotlight.

Decorative details, scale, finishes, materials, form, and historical references distinguish the Candela buildings; the same could be said of Draper's interiors, some of which endure today, such as her iconic design of the Greenbrier resort in West Virginia. In terms of day-to-day living, though, the most distinguishing features of a Candela plan are its ingenious layout and its generous size.

When these homeowners—he is one of America's most prominent businessmen; she heads her own fashion enterprise—purchased this apartment, they wanted to preserve the original layout almost exactly, yet create a new home of their own making.

What might have seemed excessive, but proved prudent, was the decision to gut the apartment and then rebuild. By "going down to

the studs," as the saying goes, the architects needed not worry about finding ways to install vital systems, such as plumbing lines, in existing terra-cotta and gypsum-block walls. Those solid walls cannot be easily opened for technical surgeries without leaving scars.

While most of the apartment's public and private rooms were recreated in their original positions, an essential change revolved around entrances and exits. Many neo-Georgian-style apartments of the 1920s and '30s featured short interior doors to preserve the double square, a reference to Palladio's list of the most harmonious proportions. So short in height were the existing doorways that the homeowners found them too formal and constraining—the rooms flowed well, but getting in and out of each felt tight. Ferguson & Shamamian expanded those openings, while shifting some closer toward the center for balance and as a way to make the spaces brighter with natural light. The team also reconfigured a warren of cramped back-of-the-house staff quarters into spacious dressing rooms and a separate office for him.

In virtually every apartment renovation, the biggest concern after determining the floorplan is the choice of finishes. The textures of walls, interior and entrance doors, moldings, floors, and window frames are the elements that uniquely define any apartment. Ferguson & Shamamian and the interior design team of Timothy Haynes and Kevin Roberts worked together to present a variety of choices to the clients, who were also intimately involved in the design process from inception. Boldface names working together in a pedigreed building might have made for some conflicts, but all parties concur that egos were checked at the actual and metaphorical door. The collaboration among the parties was fortuitous,

Left: The gallery provides direct access to all the principal rooms of the apartment. Its walls are clad in Thassos marble, while the Nero Marquina floor is bordered by nickel inlay.

Following spread: The view of the entry gallery (*left*) during construction. During demolition, the existing finishes are removed to reveal the structure, and a collaboration with the architects and builders who came before begins. The solidity of steel buried in masonry walls is exposed, and the interstitial space between the structure and the finishes is built anew to make room for new pipes, ductwork, and wiring—all in the service of modern systems.

Pages 158–159: The living room during construction. The renovation starts by acts of effacing, or the removal of outer layers. The apartment is a workshop from the day the survey is conducted until the owner moves in. It is taken over by builders, materials, and tools, all collaborating to recreate the dismantled. The work begins in a noisy mess and proceeds through gradual repairs and fixes to a conclusion of restoration and beauty as seen in the finished living room (*pages 160–161*).

Left: New window trims and profiles
from Hope's Windows are reminiscent
of 1930s New York civic buildings and
complement this building's exterior.
Below: Timothy Haynes and Kevin Roberts
convinced the homeowners to "just go
with, live with" an unconventional antique
green marble fireplace surround.

especially since the interior rebuilding and decorating
of this apartment lasted three long summers, due to
the stringent construction rules that exist for certain
Manhattan buildings, including this one.

In discussing a vocabulary for the new apartment, many
names were raised as sources of inspiration, including that
of Dorothy Draper, based on her involvement in developing
the plan of the building. During a meeting with the clients
and architects, Haynes and Roberts revealed something
that, in hindsight, feels almost prophetic. The interior
designers had in their possession (in a storage facility) the
original Steuben glass door casings they had salvaged from
the Hampshire House, the glamorous Deco-era apartment-
hotel on Central Park South whose interiors Draper also
designed. These original moldings, as well as reproductions
that were made to match, were repurposed as a fireplace
surround and door casings in the dining room. The aesthetic
spirit of Draper would prevail.

In an apartment of this scale, with views to Central
Park and a leafy side street, windows are possibly the most
noticeable element. Early in the process, the clients and
the architects were looking through different sides of the
glass. The homeowners were content with the existing
1970s-era single-pane tilt/turn windows, all twenty-eight
of them. Absent muntins and decorative hardware, the

Above: A Takashi Murakami work depicting his iconic smiling flowers
assumes a convex presence enhanced by the flat treatment of walls and ceiling in the living room.
Opposite: Reflective surfaces are combined in the dining room to sparkling effect.

Left: The steel-and-glass door of the wine cellar, which was inspired by the apartment's windows. *Right*: The lobby of Manhattan's Hampshire House, designed by Dorothy Draper, featuring moldings seen at far right. *Far right*: Original Steuben bolection molding salvaged from Hampshire House is integrated in the dining room and supplemented with reproductions by craftsmen from Mirror Fair.

Following spread: The library's design—though not its eggplant-colored lacquer—was inspired by a Frances Elkins interior for a 1931 David Adler house.

windows accomplished what they were meant to do: foster unimpeded views of the park.

Yet the contractor and architects saw something else when looking through them—aging fenestrations that would detract from the new interiors. New multipaned steel windows accented with nickel bolts were chosen; set as the windows are against white plaster walls, they function as architectural jewelry. Suddenly, the windows themselves, perhaps more than the views, became a prime interior design element. This key change, which resulted in pared-down interiors, was yet another way to reference the reductivist neoclassical exterior of the building, rather than the more ordinary neo-Georgian interiors.

The interior designers were pleased with the changes, since they reflect the characters of the homeowners—a glamorous couple involved in philanthropy, as well as the cultural and commercial life of the city. While the husband may be regarded as a bit more restrained and organized, the wife possesses an exuberant sense of color and panache. A neutral palette was the best choice for most of the apartment, where notable works by Warhol, Murakami, and other well-known artists pop as color; in contrast, the library is lacquered in a rich purple.

Although a wine room is now a common request in large houses and apartments, here the directive was more pronounced. The husband wanted a dedicated wine cellar as conspicuous as one of the apartment's park views. Ferguson & Shamamian was concerned that such a space would appear too commercial in a residence unless it were seamlessly integrated into the architecture. They fashioned a room fronted by a floor-to-ceiling steel window, a loud-and-clear echo of those found throughout the apartment. The result serves as an attractive scrim for viewing the bottles nestled in racks.

In this apartment, the spirit of Candela and Draper, the building's original personalities, remains. As for the present-day personalities—the clients, architects, and interior designers—they listened not only to the voices of their predecessors, but also to each other. Past and present came together ultimately to create something unique.

ANGLE OF REPOSE

The siting of a new house in Greenwich,
Connecticut, defined how it embraced natural light
and how the family occupies it.

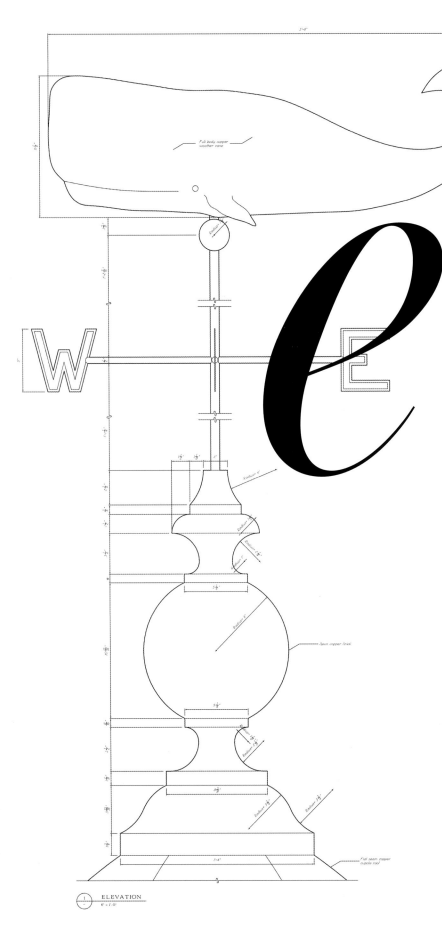

ELEVATION

Previous spread: Views of the
Long Island Sound were
important to the owners. The
most dramatic vantage point
is from the rooftop cupola and
widow's walk.

very house has its public and private identities. From the street in Greenwich's Belle Haven neighborhood, this residence assumes a handsome, symmetrical profile, indicative of a traditional Georgian–style residence. From within, however, the public and private rooms embrace views of a bucolic, undulating three-acre terrain not visible from the road.

When the European-born homeowners commissioned Ferguson & Shamamian to design a house for themselves and their three children, they wanted an American home, complete with white clapboard siding, a symmetrical form, and a sunny disposition. So intent were they on adhering to American details that they enthusiastically endorsed Ferguson & Shamamian's suggestion to top the cupola with a cast-metal weather vane in the shape of a whale.

Yet they also wanted a home that would be appropriate to its site and neighborhood and authentically detailed. On the first visit to the site, the architects encountered a large hole in the center of the property from the previously demolished house. When the Ferguson & Shamamian team members conceived the new house, they positioned it toward the front of the property as a way to open up the rest of the land for gardens and lawns. The resulting dwelling could hardly be called diminutive, but because of the way it is sited on the sloping lot, no one looking at it from the street or driveway would know the true size.

To enjoy the glorious setting where their house is positioned, the homeowners and their family can retreat to a private rooftop widow's walk, accessed via a hexagonal glassed cupola. From that windy vantage atop the residence, the blue of Long Island Sound comes into view. That contemplative outdoor space is anchored by an opposing pair of arched red-brick chimneys, the forms of which hark back to Virginia's Stratford Hall, an exemplar of eighteenth-century American-Georgian architecture. Family members can wander to lookout points by the chimney archways, each anchored in place by four pylons, and remain unseen by anyone below.

More typical of a Shingle-style house than a neo-Georgian one, this residence includes a long splayed wing set at a discreet 18-degree angle. On the first floor, that arm includes an expansive open-plan kitchen and a family room that culminates in a rounded, faceted endpoint from which occupants can take in a 360-degree view of the property.

The house that presents itself to the public is, ultimately, narrow, barely two rooms deep, with the dining and living rooms facing the rear. The resulting center-hall plan allows views from the adjacent living and dining rooms out to the spectacular gardens. Rooms downstairs and upstairs along the splayed arm are bright with natural light throughout the day, as if the sunlight is the chief decorative element.

The first drawn schemes of the house featured orthogonal wings. It was decided that right angles were wrong for a house that wanted to be symmetrical, but not too much so. When the idea for this splayed arm was agreed upon, the original plan had it positioned on the other side of

Above: A working drawing of the weather vane
for the cupola. *Opposite*: The house's position
(*foreground*) in its Greenwich neighborhood shows
its proximity to the Long Island Sound.

Left and below: The south-facing rear terrace is sheltered from direct sunlight by a grouping of London plane trees planted in the patio.

the house, but the land views there were not as dramatic, so the plan was flipped. Paramount to the homeowners (and likely to their fellow residents of the Belle Haven enclave) was that their house appear as if it had been there for well over a century, like many of the extant houses in the neighborhood. At first glance, the house does look as if it belonged to the original neighborhood, a tranquil, turn-of-the-last-century residential park noted for its small-town feel, with sidewalks, slower street speeds, and on-site security. Once inside the house, though, it is immediately apparent that its details and relatively open floorplan are not traditional. Victoria Hagan, the clients' interior designer, refers to the flow of the interiors as confidently modern, which is signaled by the ease with which family and guests can move through the many rooms.

From the start of the project, Hagan was aware of both the clients' and the firm's interest in establishing symmetry. But Hagan understood, too, that symmetry is always best when it's accented with a little something unexpected that departs from an emphatic balance. Those surprising moments occur both in the architecture and in the rooms she furnished. "Victoria is a very thoughtful designer," says Oscar Shamamian, "and she always wants to know exactly what we're doing so that she can know how it affects her design. She has an uncanny ability to connect with everyone involved on a project."

The firm fitted the pool house with shingles, a hip roof, and a rotated cupola as a way to distinguish it from the main house. This structure is situated at a distance from the main residence and appears to meld with the grounds, like a garden folly. Akin to the main house, though, it features a pair of brick chimneys and a cupola. Operative fanlights punctuate the front façade, and behind each is a changing room. These diminutive windows are not only visually attractive elements but practical ones, since they provide for air circulation and privacy.

Because scale is a key consideration for Hagan, she knew that the high ceilings in the home, coupled with the size of some of the rooms, necessitated a careful balance of proportions in the furnishings. To watch Hagan during the installation of furnishings and accessories is to witness an on-premises tailor of sorts, though she doesn't need a tape measure to know when something is off by even the smallest amount. During the install at this house, she could tell from a distance that one of the sofas was too high by a half-inch; she had the legs trimmed on the spot. She insists that interior design, especially for a project of this scale, should be considered not a science but an act of intuition.

While the house announces itself from the curb as symmetrical, perhaps even predictable, in its layout, it defies that assessment at every point, which is what makes this house so engaging. An obvious sign of the refusal to be predictable occurs at the junction of the angled arm and the main residence. There one sees a curved window, its glass actually concave, a detail rarely found in an American Colonial or Georgian-style house. That lovely, sculptural moment says that this is an original dwelling for original clients. Someday, far in the future, people will look upon this residence as the old house on the block that endured and aged well.

Previous spread, left: A butler's pantry and bar is located at the very point where the splayed wing meets the main block. *Previous spread, right*: The exterior of the crux of the wing is accentuated with a convex bay window at the first-floor pantry and a concave window on the second floor.

Above: Oversized pocket doors open to connect the family room to the breakfast room and kitchen. *Opposite*: The living room fireplace mantel with crossettes is similar to the surrounds of the arched bookcase and door.

Clockwise from above: Entry hall and stair; front portico; an early floorplan for the house was reversed in order to preserve an old sycamore tree.

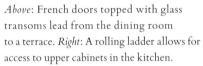
Above: French doors topped with glass transoms lead from the dining room to a terrace. *Right*: A rolling ladder allows for access to upper cabinets in the kitchen.

Left: The library is paneled in a natural cherrywood. *Above*: A custom Petit Granit mantel with bolection molding and a pulvinated frieze echoes the living room fireplace.

A FAMILY AFFAIR

As a family grew, its members
decided to build a new residence
where they could expand
and flourish far into the future.

Previous spread: Plantings in the entrance courtyard are spare. The space functions more as an outdoor room than as a garden. Operable shutters allow privacy, if desired.

Opposite: A dining pergola centers on the sinuous branches of an old sycamore tree that was preserved when the new house was built. *Below*: Symmetry and perspective at work—an axial view through the entrance courtyard to the pool pavilion.

*W*e often remember our first house most fondly. Such was the case with this owner, who, as a young man from abroad, had long ago purchased the sprawling, period-detailed Tudor-style mansion on this site in Bel Air. While living there, he completed his college studies, married, and eventually brought home his first-born son. He and his wife planted lemon trees on the property and admired the baronial rooms. But as his children grew up and he began to spend far more time overseas in his homeland, a Bel Air residence evocative of an English castle seemed inconsistent with their lifestyle.

There were other problems with the old house: its rooms were uneven; some of the bedrooms had shared bathrooms; other rooms were dark; still others were configured in unwieldly, though picturesque, ways, with towers and turrets. The adult children sought parity. They wanted a house that could grow with the family, as grandchildren arrived. They wanted seven bedrooms of equal size that were bright with natural light, each with its own bathroom, as well as rooms on the first level with ready access to a contemplative courtyard, a swimming pool, and a pool house.

A potential solution to their dilemma was to abandon the existing Tudor-style house and purchase the one next door, another house that had been completed by Ferguson & Shamamian several years earlier. Although they did not purchase that residence, they gained a deep appreciation for it, cementing the family's desire to engage the firm to build a new house.

The close-knit family had vacationed often in Tuscany and felt that a house reflective of that region and a reminder of their times spent there would suit their desires. Their dream house would feature a sunny interior courtyard with a plashing fountain, red-tiled roofs, archways, loggias, harmonious details, and classical proportions. A Tuscan-style house like the one they imagined was hardly an anomaly in Southern California, though one articulated this expertly is rare.

With a heavy heart, the father finally agreed to allow his first house to be torn down and replaced with one that was more suited to his family's needs. Upon commissioning Ferguson & Shamamian, the two demands he made for the new residence were that certain established trees would be preserved and that select fixtures from the old house would be incorporated somewhere in the new. While Tudor and Tuscan are not exactly complementary styles, they do meet here, albeit briefly, in the basement level of the new home. There, one finds Tudoresque tracery on the ceiling, paneled Jacobean doors, and fixtures typical of an English castle.

The design process was a lengthy one. The family patriarch and matriarch, along with their children, met regularly with Ferguson & Shamamian and, later, with interior designer Madeline Stuart to conceive, shape, and decide on every detail. The lengthiness was due to a shared desire for everything to be perfectly right and be done only when it was ready. Given that the family members spend a considerable amount of time abroad, some design decisions, both architectural and decorative, were accomplished remotely. Ultimately, the construction would take nearly two years. The designers and the building contractor understood that a measured, methodical approach would most successfully produce the house the client envisioned.

One of the few decisions that was made quickly, though late in the architectural design process, was that of hiring interior designer Madeline Stuart, whose work the family admired. Stuart was sensitive to, and mindful of, the fact that her late introduction into the project could prove

Above: Doorways illustrate a language both varied and consistent.
Opposite: Antique chinoiserie scenes inspired new custom wallpaper commissioned
by Madeline Stuart for the dining room.

Above: The floor and staircase at the entry are made of natural stone; the contrasting baseboards and door surround are *stuc pierre*, executed by Rex Pratt. *Opposite*: French doors in the double-height living room open to the entry courtyard, blurring the distinction between outdoor and indoor spaces.

Opposite, top to bottom: Niches in the foyer are designed to hold antique mirrors and complementary console tables; referencing classical Roman motifs, a decorative flooring pattern in the foyer creates a mosaic rug. *Above, top to bottom*: The rear loggia connects the library and dining room; the walnut-paneled library.

Previous spread: The limbs of a mature oak tree scroll across the pool pavilion, framing the view from the meditative garden to the main house.

Below: A bay window provides space for a small balcony off one of the bedrooms.
Right: Italian-inspired wood-paneled doors appear throughout the house.

potentially unsettling to the architects. Indeed, at first the two design teams eyed each other's work with a certain wariness, but they soon came together—as harmoniously as the home's classically styled proportions. Stuart emphasizes that while she was swift to produce designs for custom mosaic floors, stenciled walls, and bathroom cabinetry, she was careful not to undermine the architectural agenda already underway. Just as Stuart embraced Ferguson & Shamamian's vision for the house, so, too, did the firm welcome the spirit of her work.

The entry to the house is both ceremonious and friendly. Visitors pass through a pair of wrought-iron gates into the spacious courtyard, which affords a central view on axis through the living room to the rear loggia and pool house beyond. The courtyard functions as an outdoor room and provides access to the foyer through a single carved wooden door at the end of the east corridor, as well as to the living room through a series of French doors to the north, and, more discreetly, to the guest wing on its west corridor. The courtyard is an interpretation of such

spaces found in Italy and throughout the Mediterranean, but it is also informed by the work of American architect Philip Shutze (1890–1982), who expertly reinterpreted Classicism for an American audience. This house is set principally on an eight-foot grid. That mathematical plan carries throughout and governs the floorplan. Ceilings on the first level are mostly ten and a half feet tall, and the rooms are meant to feel spacious and airy.

In keeping with classical ideals, the architects instituted a hierarchy of ornament. The most important public rooms—living room, dining room, entry foyer, library—display the greatest amount of detail. Doorways to the living and dining rooms, for instance, are accented with pediments and friezes (made of plaster known as *stuc pierre,* which has an uncanny resemblance to limestone). The hierarchies in the home are

conveyed through its moldings. The living room is notable not only for its scale and accessibility to the outdoors, but also for its double height, the ceiling coursed by beams typical of a Tuscan villa. Punctuating the center of the room, a pair of upper windows flanks a glass door hemmed by a Juliet balcony, behind which runs a corridor connecting the bedroom suites on the second floor. The details in the house become more subtle as one goes deeper into it.

While Madeline Stuart was keen to honor the architecture in every room, she freely mixed Italian and other European antiques with Asian motifs, another particular interest of the client. The family has spent considerable time in Europe, and its members are well-versed in Continental architectural and aesthetic traditions. For the dining room, Stuart recalls bringing the wife to a dealer in New York, where they encountered antique chinoiserie panels depicting flora and fauna, water elements, and drifting clouds that elicited a collective sigh of agreement. Those scenes inspired a wallpaper design that now adorns the dining room walls, imbuing the room with serenity. In the living room hangs a pair of large square paintings of Chinese landscapes. Their mode of purchase, while by no means nefarious, was an unlikely one. An out-of-town art dealer representing the sale had no gallery space and could meet only on the street in New York City. The dealer arrived in a van, removed the valuable paintings from the back, and displayed them against his truck for Stuart and her client. The decision to purchase was made then and there on the sidewalk with many a passerby stopping to admire the canvases and nod their approval.

When the house was completed, the homeowners invited the architects and Stuart to a celebration, following a private blessing. Gathered among the family members and their friends, the architects were reminded, yet again, that the most gratifying moment in designing any home is bearing witness to a family actually living in it and enjoying it.

THE FULL RANGE

A couple commissioned a stone house in Aspen that would both stand out from and be an integral part of the landscape.

Previous spread: Timber, stone, steel, and glass at home in the mountains.

Left: Beams supporting delicate barrel vaults in the foyer are a prelude to larger volumes inside and the expansive views to come. *Right*: In the living room, the exposed Douglas fir timbers showcase the underside of the roof.

Following spread: The panoramic drama of Aspen Mountain framed by a heavy timber screen is enjoyed year-round from the open-air loggia.

ountains are not inert. They have life, especially the ones in Aspen. Their solidity belies the fact that they change color throughout the day. The leaves, the bark, the canopies of the aspens and evergreens that beard the lower reaches of the mountains change, season to season, morning to night. Snows build and ebb as if by tidal forces. And many slopes are alive with skiers, brought up in chairlifts that swing in the wind. From the right vantage, the slopes and ridges of the Rocky Mountains appear as a kind of ongoing movie, whose stars are skiers and natural forces. There is not a moment in this house when that cinematic dynamic is not acknowledged. Every room has unimpeded views of the mountains that define Aspen. The finished design, inside and out, is the result of the architects, interior designers, and homeowners recognizing that the beauty of Aspen warrants viewing in full color.

Like an incipient skier, though, Ferguson & Shamamian had a few false starts early in the design process. The initial designs envisioned a traditional ski lodge, but the owners suggested otherwise, bringing reference images of more modern houses with large expanses of glass and minimalist interiors. A second attempt drew the designs toward the modern, to which the homeowners responded, "You're not getting it."

But beginner skiers eventually find their footing and balance, as did this team. Working closely with the homeowners, and interior designers Bunny Williams and Elizabeth Lawrence, resulted in a synthesis. Just as Ferguson & Shamamian responded to directives for a more contemporary style, so, too, did the homeowners begin to understand the need for more traditional materials and forms. Williams and Lawrence confide that well into their work, they detected the couple's shift toward furnishings and decorative details more suitable to traditional interiors than spare ones. The homeowners realized, too, upon viewing various versions from the architects, that a house in—and of—the mountains needs to respond to those surrounding natural forms rather than retreat from them. A house here needs sinuous forms, vigorous materials, and solidity to complement the peaks. The design team landed on Belgian and Provençal styles. The materials used, including Douglas fir and stone quarried from Napa Valley, were the signposts that led to a concerted design.

When building houses in Aspen, one contends with steep grades. Topography is the first challenge, though it can also be a primary advantage. The noble profiles of the mountains demand an equally grand gesture of a house, all in appropriate scale. The mountains dictated what to configure, namely, an "upside-down" house, in the sense that the public living areas

Clockwise across spread from top left: South face of the house among autumnal aspens; heavy timber brackets frame a lighter screen of glass and wood at the entry door; another view of the loggia with glass-and-metal doors that open on a path to the pool; detail of rafters at roof overhang; a stone and plaster range hood draws the eye up to the beamed ceiling in the kitchen.

Following spread, left: One of the house's varied elaborations of exposed timber
ceiling in the dining room. *Following spread, right*: The grandeur of the mountain peaks is echoed by the
sloped ceiling in the main bedroom.

Previous spread: Local Rocky Mountain flora and fauna along the road to town on a crisp fall day.

Below: The pool terrace firepit is at the highest point on the property, equal in elevation with the roof of the house, and is the perfect place for sunset views.
Right: Framing the magnificent view of the mountains, steel windows and doors in the library lead to the rear terrace.

and main suite are situated on the ground level, where one enters the house, while the remaining two floors of bedrooms and other private rooms are downstairs. The lowest level includes a wine cellar, a home theater, a gym, and bunkrooms. With the exception of the bunkrooms, which are lit with natural light via areaway windows, the rooms are windowless; mirrored walls in the gym help mitigate the effect in a space that might otherwise feel as dark as a mineshaft.

In so configuring the house, views to the mountains were captured in cinematic glory. To occupy any of the rooms and gaze out the windows is, in a sense, to watch a film taking place throughout the day. The homeowners often remark that their favorite time in the house is at night, when the groomers are tending the slopes and their lights twinkle among the trees. But then there is the special moment in the day, too, when shadows on the mountains move with epic scale.

Once the style of the house was agreed upon, Williams and Lawrence began to hone the interiors. It's a common—and often meaningless—phrase in interior design to say that the rooms of a home are "timeless," in that they don't reveal a decor particular to a certain time and place. But that goal was of special concern to all of the parties. Both the architecture and interior design were to suit a house rooted in today while remaining relevant for tomorrow.

Aspen is deeply respectful of its nature. When building there, one must follow stringent regulations, from exterior light selections that minimize light pollution to the height of the homes in relation to nearby hillsides. Such restrictions informed the shape of this house from the beginning.

Scale was another key consideration. Here was yet another opportunity for Ferguson & Shamamian to indulge not only in size but also in detail, notably with the ceilings—some coffered, others coursed by massive beams, and still others with rhythmic plaster barrel arches vaulting between beams. Rafter tails, visible on both the interior and exterior, are structural. Williams and Lawrence knew that the furnishings would need to relate to the tall interior spaces, while also responding to mountain elevations that reach up thousands of feet.

Ferguson & Shamamian suggested windows composed of multiple muntins and panes of glass, which would give scale and enhance views, while heightening the intimacy of the interiors. By dividing windows with muntins, the natural and dramatic stories outside these windows, as well as that of the picturesque town of Aspen, were captured in frames. Ferguson & Shamamian were strong advocates of windows with multiple divisions in order to give those views scale. "We struggled with this decision about the windows," admits the husband, "but we came to realize that having the panes would let us really witness the way Aspen changes throughout the day—from morning to sunset to evening when the lights come on in town."

Just as a house makes a first impression from the curb, it makes a second impression from the threshold. Williams and Lawrence recognize that first moment in the house as one to exploit to its fullest. That initial introduction to the interior of a house is, as Lawrence says, "exciting and it alerts people to what to expect throughout—in the architecture and decor. An interior designer has to think about these moments and make them work." Here, Williams and Lawrence positioned a pair of benches with sinuous lines on either side of the front door; these items of furniture, at once modern and traditional, serve as a tip-off to the tenor of the house as a whole.

Among the most memorable rooms is the covered patio, or loggia, made usable year-round by the fireplace and heating lamps installed near the rafters. The room, as much a part of the outdoors as the indoors, features numerous focal points—the vigorously articulated stone wall, the fireplace, the engaging pattern of beams and rafters, and, best of all, the glow of Aspen below. That view alone will keep this house timeless; it will never grow old. Architecture and decor work in concert here to take in the natural drama that is Aspen.

While the windows of the house look out, screenlike, the structure is more than a mere viewer in the audience: it's one of the stars of the show.

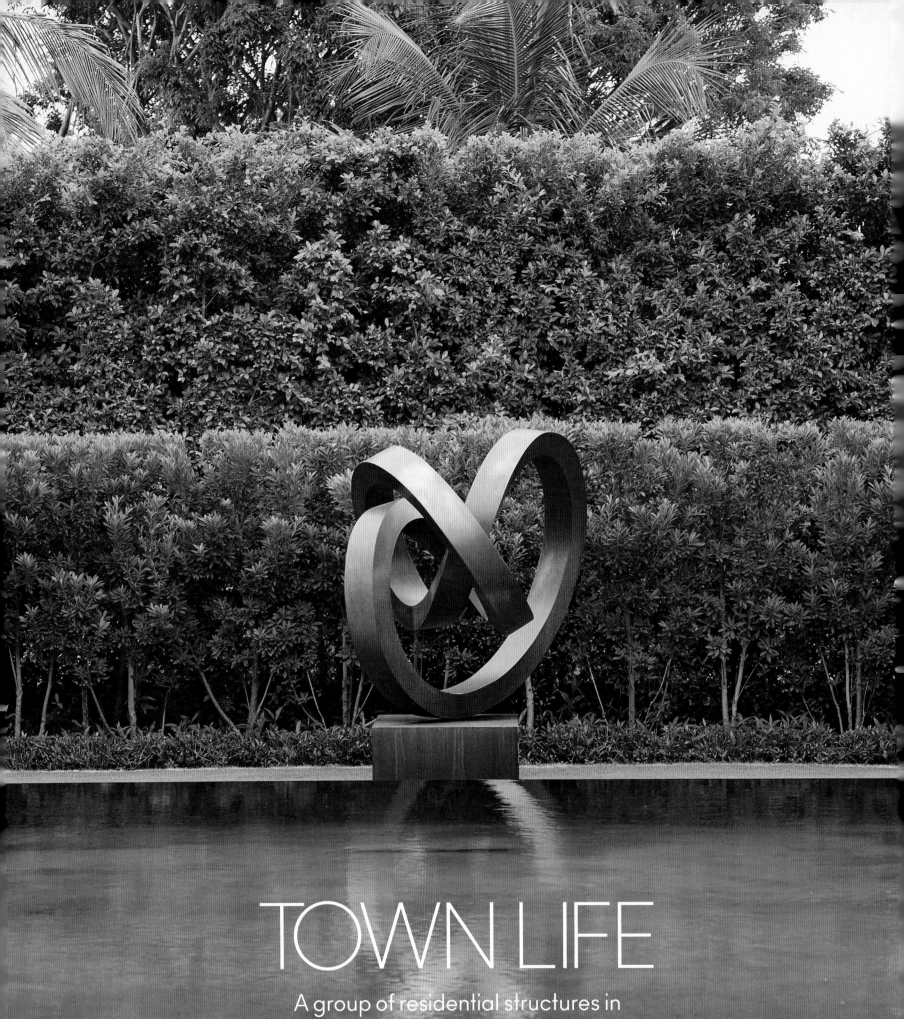

TOWN LIFE

A group of residential structures in
Palm Beach becomes a village, a private enclave
within an established neighborhood.

Previous spread, left: A tall, sculpted hedge creates a secluded outdoor room at the pool while hiding the street behind it. Gino Miles's bronze kinetic sculpture turns in the breeze before a layered green backdrop. *Previous spread, right*: Set deep within the property, a single door through a garden wall leads into a small courtyard with access to all rooms.

Left: The architects carefully orchestrate the entry progression that begins at the reserved street façade and builds through the house. *Right*: Mark Ferguson's early elevation studies express a compact house.

*f*or many residents of Palm Beach, one of the most appealing aspects of the town is its density. While many of its spacious homes are set on ample lots, no one is ever far from one another. Houses, apartments, storefronts, hotels, and public buildings all intermingle. There is a strong sense of community, of town life, wherever one goes in Palm Beach.

And that is why this assemblage of residential structures is a microcosm of the best feature of Palm Beach. The homeowners commissioned Ferguson & Shamamian to build a new main house on an empty lot; a pool and pool house on an adjacent lot that required the removal of an existing ranch house; and the renovation of an extant house into guest quarters on a third site. Other elements include a garage and a series of alluring garden allées. These separate properties combine to produce a larger effect, an important dynamic given that the clients all along had wanted a house of modest scale, unprepossessing both from the curb and inside. The result is a village of structures, a neighborhood of buildings enveloped by a pink wall within an established, tranquil Palm Beach neighborhood.

The husband is a builder. Not only is he known as a commissioner of homes that he and his wife occupy, but he has also amassed an extensive collection of architectural drawings so important that museums have mounted exhibitions of the works. "What I care about is architecture and its details," he emphasizes. Interior designer Bunny Williams, who has decorated six of the couple's residences over more than three decades, recalls telling the husband that he should have been an architect instead of a businessman, whereupon he replied with characteristic humor, "If I'd done that, I couldn't have afforded to have built all of my houses."

He is, indeed, "a master builder," a term that Ferguson & Shamamian founding partner Mark Ferguson attributes to him. Sites so inspire the owner, according to Ferguson, that "he always begins a new project with a clear vision. He knows where the house belongs on the site, where key rooms will enjoy the best views, where the house will flow between indoors and outdoors, and the qualities needed to make a welcoming and comfortable place."

This project was inspired by a morning walk. The husband's routine includes a stroll along the Palm Beach Lake Trail. During his forays, he often would pause at an empty corner lot to which he had such a strong response that he envisioned building a new home there, despite the lot's small size. He bought the land and eventually purchased two adjacent properties. In conceiving the new residence with Ferguson & Shamamian and Williams, he wanted it to embody his personal architectural passions. He envisioned the new house as one composed of several parts, a compendium of the past and a compilation of all the styles and forms he has admired and wishes to live among, from Beaux-Arts to Mediterranean.

While the homeowners wanted the property to accomplish a lot, personally and architecturally, the sites were constrained, with one side bordered by a tall apartment building. Ferguson & Shamamian's role was to maximize the full site, while ensuring that water views remained visible from the main rooms of the main house. Also, the team had to find a way to build multiple structures that would relate to one another on two plots but would be distinctive in form and function.

Having previously designed a house in Connecticut and an apartment in the San Remo in Manhattan for the couple, Ferguson & Shamamian knew instinctively the style the clients would want for their new Palm Beach residence: Mediterranean. While Palm Beach is defined by many elements— social, climatic, architectural—its signature Mediterranean-style buildings are its most conspicuous. A drive along any of the town's streets reveals its prevalence in residences, public buildings, hotels, and stores. Red-tiled

West Elevation

North Elevation

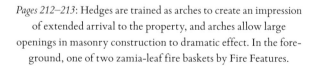

Pages 212–213: Hedges are trained as arches to create an impression of extended arrival to the property, and arches allow large openings in masonry construction to dramatic effect. In the foreground, one of two zamia-leaf fire baskets by Fire Features.

Previous spread, left: In the living room, a broad expanse of smooth plaster wall is punctuated by a coquina door surround separating public areas from private. Previous spread, right: On the opposite wall, the unarticulated arches maintain visual connections and allow direct transitions to rooms beyond.

Above: A vaulted ceiling in the foyer is a moment of compression before entering the living room. Right: Accordion folding doors on both sides of the living room create three distinct yet connected spaces, allowing light, air, and the water view into the center of the house.

roofs, courtyards, white-stucco exteriors, arcades, arched windows and entryways, and Juliet balconies are found everywhere in town. Both the owners and the architectural team were committed to building a home consistent with the location that would enhance the community. So successful was the project in that regard that the Preservation Foundation of Palm Beach awarded the house its Schuler Award, recognizing the residence's contribution to the town's architectural heritage. Appropriate extant styles make for good neighbors.

It is one of the ironies of Florida that a sunny, warm climate so conducive to outdoor living can also keep many residents indoors with humming air-conditioning. This couple loves the outdoors, however, and wanted a home configured around a central courtyard that embraced the dynamic of indoor/outdoor living. Ferguson & Shamamian wisely positioned the pool on the street side to address issues of privacy, given the apartment building to the north. While the house and the other structures maximize their site, abundant natural light and air prevail, inside and out, an effect fostered by vaulted ceilings, large windows, and a repeating series of arched French doorways. Landscape designer Mario Nievera was brought into the project to transform the outdoor spaces

into outdoor rooms with not only furniture but also appropriate plantings. Nievera's landscape designs respond to architecture. For the modern houses in Palm Beach where he has worked, his plantings are sparer, more geometric; for the Mediterranean style, his plantings are lush, evocative of tropical jungles. Precise and alluring pathways cut through the dense greenery.

Given the owners' wishes for unimpeded views from every window, Ferguson & Shamamian struggled with the solid-to-void ratio, that key dynamic in architecture in which a balance is struck between the mass of a building and its openings. To remain faithful to the vocabulary of masonry construction requires piercing the envelope with a sufficient number of windows and doors for light and views, but not so many or such large openings as to undermine the solidity and weight of a sheltering structure. Here was

an instance where a compromise needed to be made. The clients wanted to enjoy expansive views from inside, while the architects wanted thick, sturdy load-bearing masonry walls and cool shady interiors, typical of the Mediterranean tradition, to be the distinguishing feature of the buildings. Architectural character is more than skin-deep.

The wife, in particular, was reluctant to have yet another large house among their residences. She wanted this new one to be spacious enough, but not oversized. Indeed, no single structure in this collection of buildings is large, but in the aggregate the compound is more than ample.

In terms of architectural detail, there is plenty to admire—in the living room alone are massive oak rafters, carved beams, and purlins, all supported by decorative corbels. Rusticated brick vaults run, wave-like, along the kitchen ceiling, bearing on salvaged barn beams. At the entryway, Ferguson & Shamamian fashioned a sculptural series of layered archways, which Ferguson describes as a "concatenation of stone arches, adapting a characteristic Byzantine motif to give a welcoming presence and architectural dignity to the front door."

Bunny Williams cites the adaptability of the interiors to any style of furnishings. In fact, she and the clients were happy to use existing furniture and accessories that they had kept in storage; what was (semi) old now looks fresh. To ensure that every piece stands out, Williams limited her palette to clear, light, natural hues; as she bluntly states, "In bright Florida, muddy colors look dead. I avoid them."

As a prolific builder of homes for himself and his wife, the owner relies on his collaborators, who have become, over these many years, not merely professional contacts but friends. Conversations among these friends result in satisfying, finished buildings. He talks readily and repeatedly of the joy he and his wife feel living in this home and how, upon walking out in the morning and crossing the loggias and terraces to reach the pool next door, he feels as if he has traversed a village. He leaves his house every day, yet remains at home.

Left: The front of the pool house is sheltered by a
pergola molded to resemble carved wood, providing
a classic weaving of garden and architecture.
Top and above: The lattice ceiling and tent valance in the pool
house create the illusion of an airy gazebo.

Following spread: Accordion doors invoke nostalgia
for a time before air-conditioning. The cool, shady room
opens fully to the outdoors.

221

KINDRED SPIRITS

A French woman envisioned an
American home true to its region in the country
she has adopted as her own.

Previous spread: Landscape designer Miranda Brooks guided the siting of the house and outbuildings on a thirty-five-acre property in Connecticut. Here, a view of the rear façade of the main house, with the pool house (*right*) and a guesthouse (*left*).

Below, left to right: A glimpse of the pool house through the kitchen garden. The distinctive front door knocker, composed of intertwining serpents, was chosen by the homeowner.
Right: One of the horses, Flair, makes an appearance at the drawing room door.

Shortly after this client inherited a château in her native France, she felt a desire for an American equivalent in Connecticut. Not a regal residence that bespeaks nobility, but one that would honor its democratic American locale. Her husband was American and her children had been born here, so she developed a deep, lasting bond with this country. Despite what her family château may suggest, she is modest. Many people involved in the design and construction of her house refer to her as spiritual.

Indeed, she feels a profound connection not only to the land her house now occupies, but also to the menagerie of animals she has brought to live on it—horses housed in their own six-stall stable, goats, miniature donkeys, dogs, and cats. Also indicative of her spiritual roots is a labyrinth she had landscape designer Miranda Brooks configure that replicates a medieval design; upon navigating it, one is said to reach a certain contemplative state. Meanwhile, nearby, the words to a Native American poem are spelled out in Morse code via a planting of boxwoods (dots) and yews (dashes). The client has been actively involved, too, in the preservation of a Revolutionary-era cemetery on her land, recognizing that she is not the first to occupy these fields.

The building of this house began during a conversation the client had with Tino Zervudachi, her Paris-based interior designer. He, in turn, introduced her to Ferguson & Shamamian, recognizing that what she wanted was exactly what the firm could deliver—houses, as she says, that are historically accurate. He also introduced her to Brooks, knowing that his client and Brooks share a mutual reverence for spiritual matters. At a

later point, when all of the parties were harmoniously collaborating on the client's home, the interior designer and principal architect shared the train back to Manhattan. During the ride, the two traded ideas and imagined a narrative of how the house might have evolved so as to inform how the rooms should look—forms taking shape as the train sped along the tracks.

The client is gracious and decisive and knew from inception how she wanted to live in the house and how the thirty-five acres could best be utilized for riding and roaming (a prime consideration for purchasing this property). Brooks took advantage of what is referred to casually in geological terms as "glacial drag," the phenomenon whereby advancing and retreating glaciers leave behind remnants. The detritus of boulders and rocks, many moss- and lichen-covered and peeking through the ground on the property, was integrated into the project. Many of the stones used for the house were gathered from the surrounding woods, as well as regional quarries. Most importantly, Brooks was instrumental in siting the house. While sitting on the land by herself one day, she decided that the new house should be located well away from the road and positioned facing southward rather than east, as the previous house had been. The client and architects readily concurred with her suggestion.

Despite the client's decisiveness, the design process took a full year and a half. The existing house had to be demolished. The new house needed to be designed, as did a variety of outbuildings, including the stable where elaborate ceiling trusses contribute to a holy, churchlike presence.

Left: The entry floor features repurposed seventeenth-century limestone pavers; the paneling references early eighteenth-century Georgian and early American patterns.
Below, top to bottom: The main staircase features cast-iron balustrades; view from the drawing room into the entrance hall.

Following spread: In keeping with the notion of an old house that has been added on to over the years, the drawing room is meant to feel as if it was once an open-air loggia, now enclosed.

Previous spread, left: The interior design for the library began with the purchase of a nineteenth-century mantelpiece and fireplace surround. The Regency style was invoked with a barrel-vault ceiling to embrace this eclectic addition; hand-painted decoration designed by Tino Zervudachi enhances the form. *Previous spread, right*: A custom sofa fills a bay window.

Above, top to bottom: A first floor guestroom; the dressing table and vanity in the main bathroom by sculptor Manuela Zervudachi. *Right*: The distinctive shape of the main bedroom ceiling results from the exterior roof lines.

Previous spread, left: The conservatory captures the last sunlight every afternoon,
especially in winter. The floor, designed by Tino Zervudachi, is fashioned of
matte terracotta and glossy Spanish tiles. *Previous spread, right*: Antique French terracotta
flooring, hand-finished gray marble wainscoting, and a flower sink in the mudroom.

Opposite: Steel accordion doors allow the pool house to open fully to the terrace.
Above: The pool house is meant to evoke a farm shed.

French châteaux come with stories, given their long timelines. New American houses need to develop plots. In this case, a history was jump-started by the architects. The idea was to design a house made to look as if it had occupied its land since the early 1800s, with locally hewn stonework, massive timbers, and a later Georgian profile. A cadence of dormers defines the main portion of the house, while gabled wings appear to have been added over time. Ferguson & Shamamian purposely fostered a slight asymmetry to suggest a modest beginning and also further the idea of a house that had long been in place but onto which wings and rooms, dormers and bay windows had been added. Long, low-rising stone walls function as visual boundaries, as well as suggestions of former buildings that once stood there. The kitchen occupies what would seem to be the oldest part of the house.

As for the floorplan, the client made the surprising decision to forgo a dining room altogether. She disliked the typical layout of a living room to one side of an entry hall and a dining room to the other; nor did she want a suburban-style great room. She did know that she would occupy the principal rooms in the house every day. The drawing room includes a designated dining area, as she stipulated; the library evokes in its colors and wood-work a room in Ireland's Lismore Castle, a favorite of the homeowner's; a year-round conservatory functions much like an orangerie, complete with fruit-bearing trees; the kitchen, with an eating nook configured in a bay window, has a more country feel to it, akin to that in her residence in France; and a screened porch functions as a year-round dining spot, with windows easily installed off-season.

A transitional butler's pantry linking the kitchen and drawing room needed to be both visually and architecturally engaging. For the space, Zervudachi positioned an eighteenth-century English Regency mahogany cabinet, which functions as more than a repository for china and silver-ware. He proposed that the paneling be designed to frame the cabinet as a way to blend it with the architecture.

The homeowner also wanted the stair hall to be spacious enough to highlight her collection of art, a body of works that truly merits that much overused term "eclectic." Zervudachi had the walls painted a shade called Hague Blue, an apt description for the moody hue against which hang a stellar collection of Old Master Dutch still lifes—somber, contemplative, symbol-laden paintings that take on new meaning with every glance. Also filling a portion of the entrance area wall is a glimmering abstract tapestry composed of soda-bottle tops by the contemporary Ghanaian artist El Anatsui.

Zervudachi used bold, saturated swaths of color elsewhere in the house. A guest bedroom sports two tones—a dark green and a sun-bright yellow, with the windows accented with curtains featuring a sun-flower motif. That corner room is situated on the ground floor, with views to one of many gardens, thus the colors and patterns. A bar area off the library features deep gray velvet on the walls, a hue suggestive, too, of Dutch Golden Age interiors. Kitchen backsplashes are composed of vibrant mosaics, evocative of ancient designs found in places like Pompeii. Look closely enough at these surfaces and phrases emerge, in Latin and French, sentiments about food and entertaining that the client often invokes (e.g., the Latin *Bonum vinum laetificat cor hominis,* or "A good wine gladdens a person's heart").

As with all their projects, Ferguson & Shamamian emphasizes the requirement that architects need to listen to their clients. "You learn to ask questions and hear the responses, but not to be too probing," Oscar Shamamian says. "Be attentive to what else the client wants without it being stated." Here, the architects discerned the homeowner's desire to build a world around her infused with existential meaning. The architects, the interior designer, and the landscape architect were all aware that she was fashioning a place in which she could move on to her next chapters. The very materials of the house bespeak the client's desire for permanence. It's not going anywhere. Here the client is, and remains, at home.

Clockwise across spread, from top left: Rustic wooden gates were designed by Miranda Brooks and composed of branches found in the woods of the property; the garage viewed from the newly planted vegetable garden; boulders salvaged from the excavation were positioned on the land by the owner and Brooks; the meditation labyrinth is dedicated to a Native American poem that begins, "With beauty before me I walk . . ."

Previous spread, left: Newly planted hornbeam will grow into an arched green tunnel through one of the gardens. Bearded irises and Abyssinian gladioli sprout from the hoggin; *Previous spread, right*: The dining terrace with metal pergola designed by Brooks. The terrace is shaded by handmade willow mats until the wisteria grows.

Above: As seen outside the main house mudroom, traditional forms, motifs, and materials are prevalent. A number of stones used on the house and garden walls were found on the property and in the surrounding countryside.

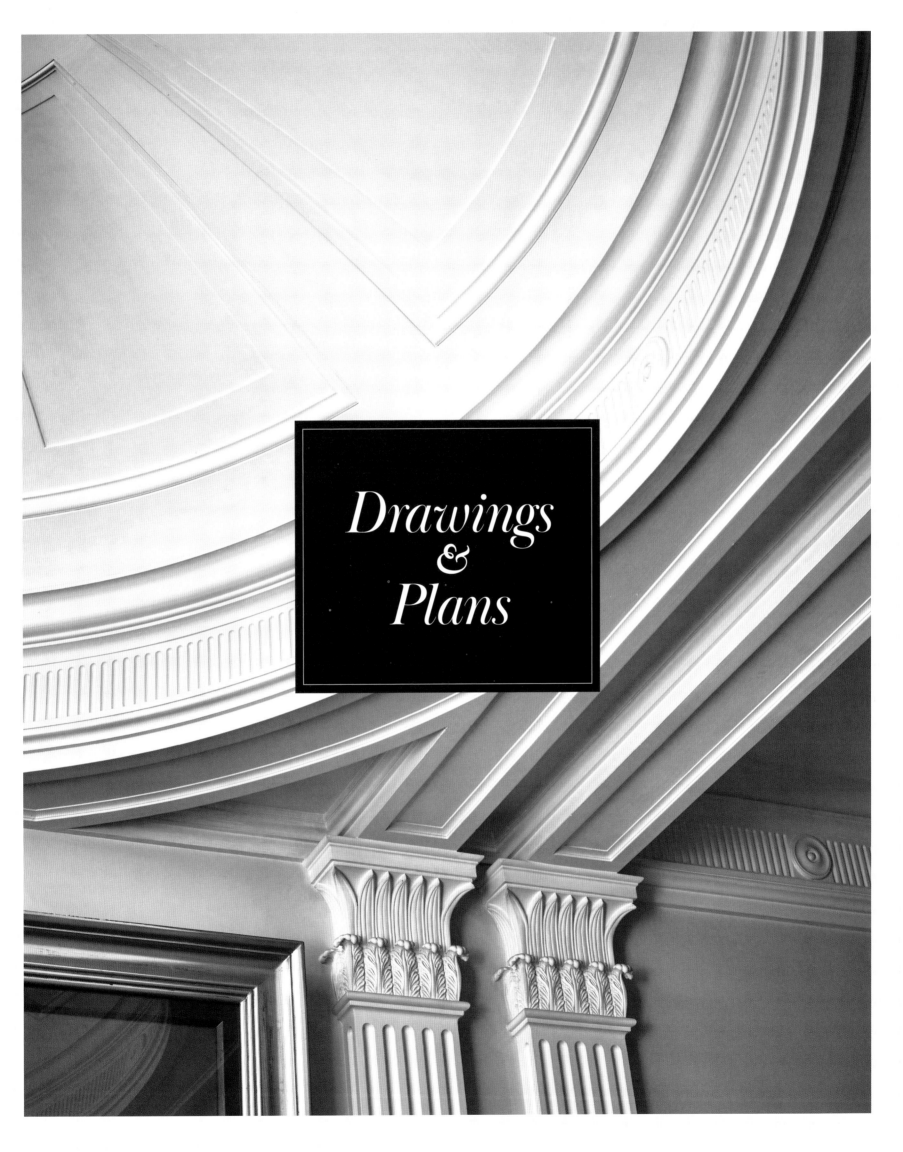

Drawings
&
Plans

East Hampton, New York, pages 18–35

Above: South elevation materials study in colored pencil by Joseph Zvejnieks
Below: Living room and dining room perspective rendering in pencil by Arthur Dutton

---

F&S TEAM
Oscar Shamamian
Stephen Chrisman
Benjamin Hatherell
Jonathan Hogg
Richard Williams
Lauren Mitchell
Marc Rehman
Ryan Inman
Michael Juckiewicz

INTERIOR DESIGN
Michael S. Smith, Inc.

LANDSCAPE DESIGN
Arne Maynard Garden Design

CONTRACTOR
Taconic Builders

ENGINEERS
Silman, structural
CES Engineering, mechanical,
electrical, plumbing

ADDITIONAL COLLABORATORS
Bruce O'Brien, New York Quarries, masonry
Cousins Furniture, millwork
Architectural Timber and Millwork, beams and timbers
Reilly Architectural, windows
Les Métalliers Champenois, metalwork
Steve Beattie Painting, decorative painting
Peter Schlesinger, metal mural

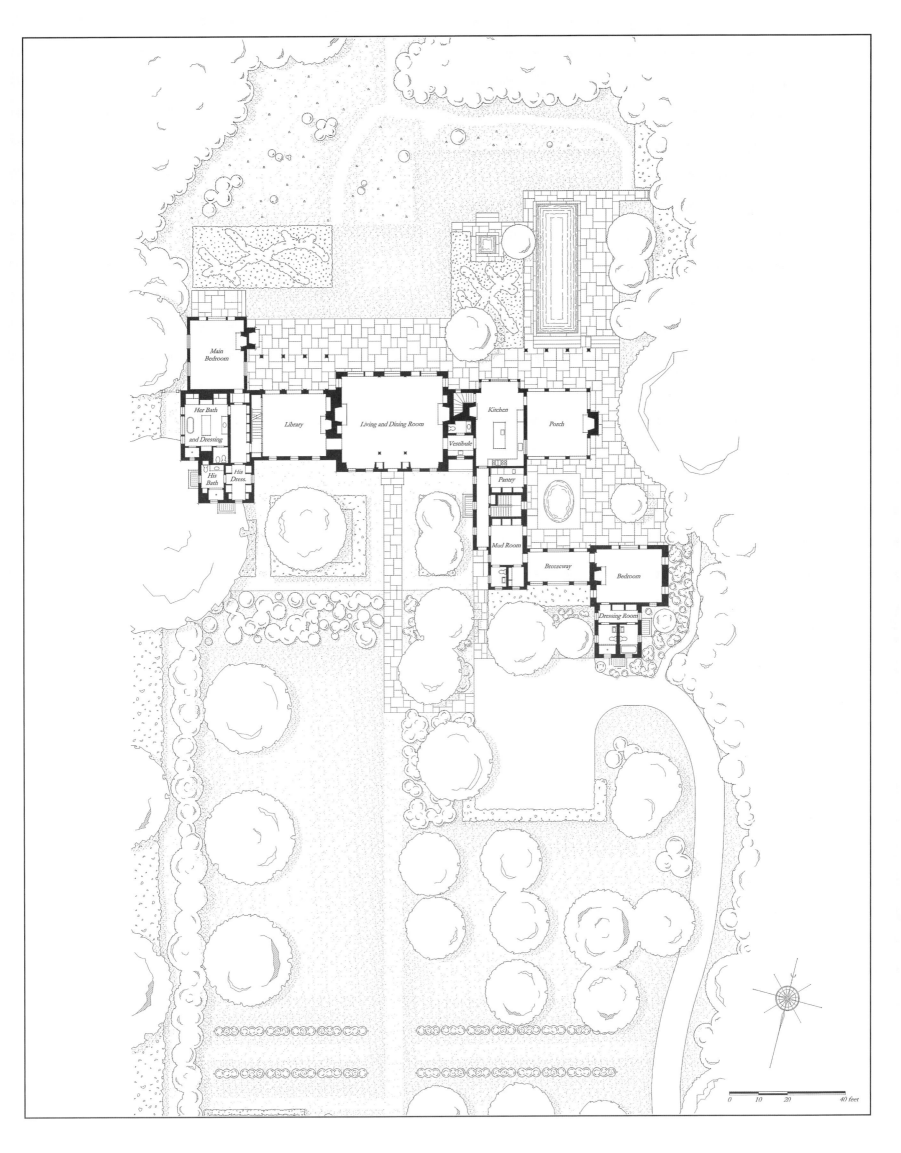

Main
Bedroom

Her Bath
and Dressing

His Dress.

His
Bath

Library

Living and Dining Room

Vestibule

Kitchen

Pantry

Porch

Mud Room

Breezeway

Bedroom

Dressing Room

0   10   20   40 feet

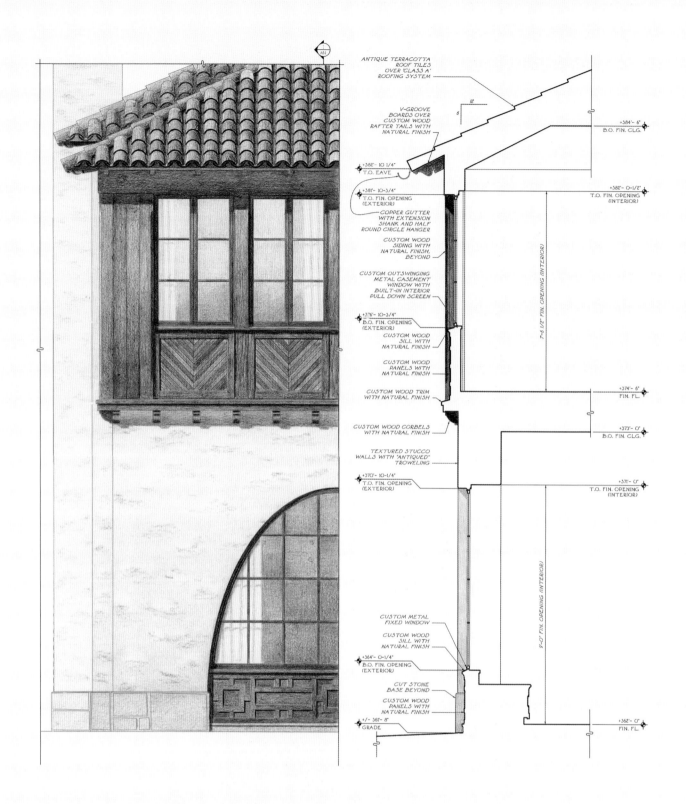

Image labels (top to bottom, architectural wall section):

ANTIQUE TERRACOTTA ROOF TILES OVER 'CLASS A' ROOFING SYSTEM

V-GROOVE BOARDS OVER CUSTOM WOOD RAFTER TAILS WITH NATURAL FINISH

+384'- 6"
B.O. FIN. CLG.

+382'- 10 1/4"
T.O. EAVE

+381'- 10-3/4"
T.O. FIN. OPENING (EXTERIOR)

COPPER GUTTER WITH EXTENSION SHANK AND HALF ROUND CIRCLE HANGER

+382'- 0-1/2"
T.O. FIN. OPENING (INTERIOR)

CUSTOM WOOD SIDING WITH NATURAL FINISH, BEYOND

CUSTOM OUTSWINGING METAL CASEMENT WINDOW WITH BUILT-IN INTERIOR PULL DOWN SCREEN

7'-4 1/2" FIN. OPENING (INTERIOR)

+376'- 10-3/4"
B.O. FIN. OPENING (EXTERIOR)

CUSTOM WOOD SILL WITH NATURAL FINISH

CUSTOM WOOD PANELS WITH NATURAL FINISH

CUSTOM WOOD TRIM WITH NATURAL FINISH

+374'- 6"
FIN. FL.

CUSTOM WOOD CORBELS WITH NATURAL FINISH

+373'- 0"
B.O. FIN. CLG.

TEXTURED STUCCO WALLS WITH "ANTIQUED" TROWELING

+370'- 10-1/4"
T.O. FIN. OPENING (EXTERIOR)

+371'- 0"
T.O. FIN. OPENING (INTERIOR)

9'-0" FIN. OPENING (INTERIOR)

CUSTOM METAL FIXED WINDOW

CUSTOM WOOD SILL WITH NATURAL FINISH

+364'- 0-1/4"
B.O. FIN. OPENING (EXTERIOR)

CUT STONE BASE BEYOND

CUSTOM WOOD PANELS WITH NATURAL FINISH

+/- 361'- 8"
GRADE

+362'- 0"
FIN. FL.

Santa Monica, California, pages 36–49

Elevation and wall section materials study in colored pencil by Joseph Zvejnieks

---

F&S TEAM
Oscar Shamamian
Thomas McManus
Justin Ford
Curtis Gibbs
Louise LeGardeur
Brent Fairbairn
Tod Elliot

ASSOCIATE ARCHITECT
Kovac Design Studio

INTERIOR DESIGN
Michael S. Smith, Inc.

LANDSCAPE DESIGN
Inner Gardens

CONTRACTOR
MG Partners

ENGINEERS
Parker Resnick
Structural Engineering,
structural
South Coast Engineering
Group, mechanical, electrical,
plumbing

ADDITIONAL COLLABORATORS
Paul Martin Tile and Stone, interior stone
Orange County Stone, masonry
Expressions in Wood; Eurotech Cabinets;
Silver Strand, Inc., millwork
Steelworks Etc., glass and steel windows and doors
Rex J. Pratt, plasterwork
Perez Brothers Iron Works, ornamental metalwork
Phillippe Anthonioz, custom brass lighting
J. Michael Designs, leaded glass, specialty glazing
Pashupatina, custom door hardware

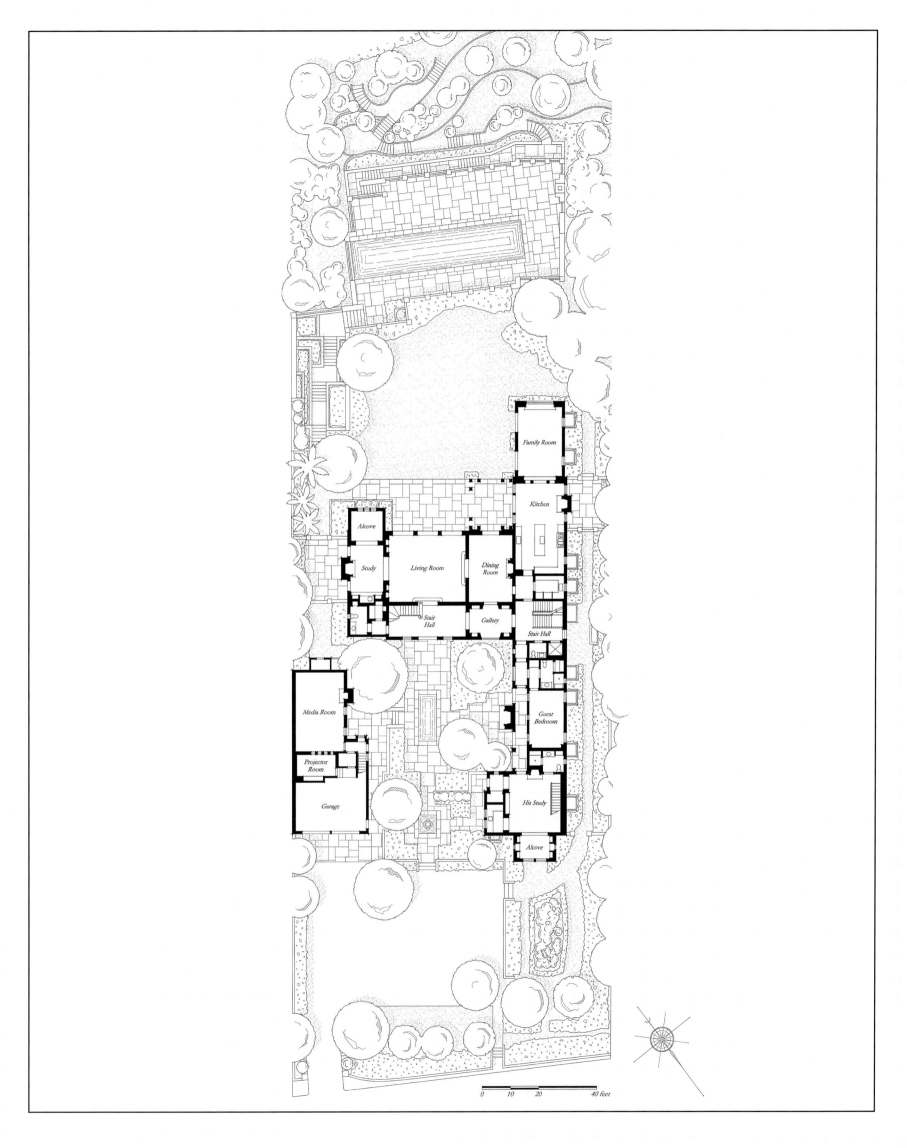

Family Room

Kitchen

Alcove

Study

Living Room

Dining
Room

Stair
Hall

Gallery

Stair Hall

Media Room

Guest
Bedroom

Projector
Room

Garage

His Study

Alcove

0   10   20   40 feet

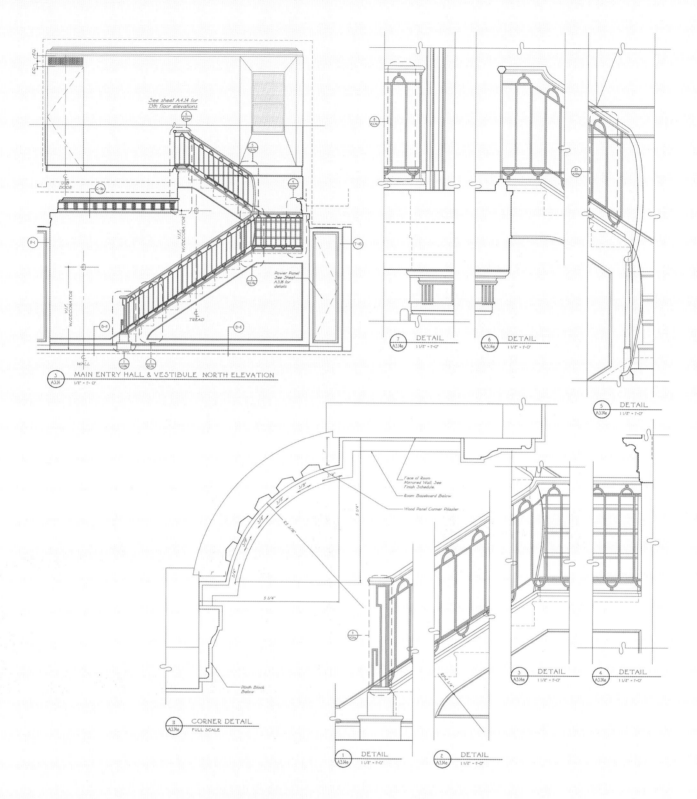

New York, New York, pages 50–67

Elevations, sections, and details of new stair

F&S TEAM
Oscar Shamamian
Brian Covington
Jonathan Hogg
Richard Williams
Marc Rehman
Ryan Inman
David Eastman

INTERIOR DESIGN
Michael S. Smith, Inc.

LANDSCAPE DESIGN
New York Garden Design

CONTRACTOR
Lico Contracting

ENGINEERS
Silman, structural
CES Engineering, mechanical,
electrical, plumbing

ADDITIONAL COLLABORATORS
Precision Stone; A&G Marble; DaVinci
Stone, interior stone
Hyde Park Mouldings, plasterwork
Féau et Cie, paneling
La Forge De Style, door and railing metalwork
Boyd Reath, gilding and gold/silver leaf
Miriam Ellner, églomisé
Nancy Lorenz, breakfast room metal wall treatment
H. Theophile, custom door hardware

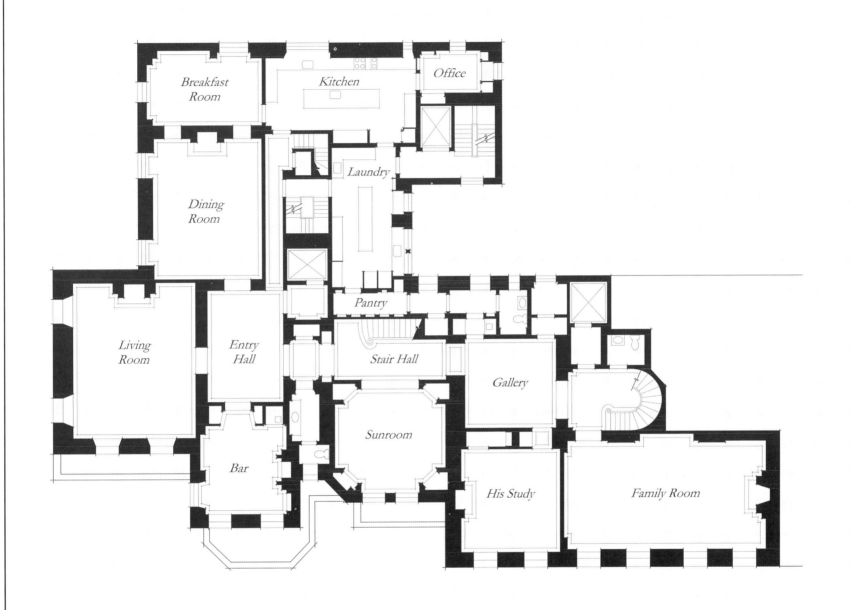

Breakfast Room

Kitchen

Office

Dining Room

Laundry

Living Room

Entry Hall

Stair Hall

Pantry

Gallery

Sunroom

Bar

His Study

Family Room

71st Street

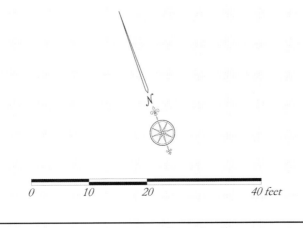

N

0   10   20   40 feet

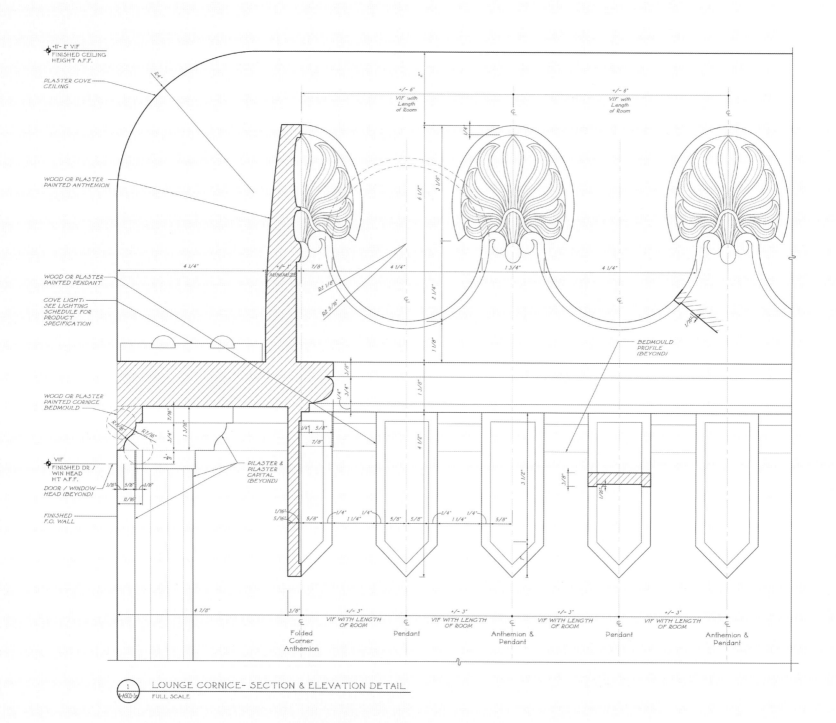

LOUNGE CORNICE- SECTION & ELEVATION DETAIL
FULL SCALE

Downeast Maine, pages 68–89

Working drawing of illuminated cove and cornice in playhouse nightclub

---

F&S TEAM
Mark Ferguson
Scott Sottile
Soledad Méndez
William Rutledge
Lea Teitelbaum
Joseph Mancino
Race Alexander

INTERIOR DESIGN
Nina Campbell Interiors

LANDSCAPE DESIGN
Deborah Nevins & Associates

CONTRACTOR
Nate Holyoke Builders

ENGINEERS
Silman, structural
CES Engineering, mechanical,
electrical, plumbing

ADDITIONAL COLLABORATORS
Freshwater Stone & Brickwork; Harkins
Masonry, masonry
Canova & Stone, millwork
Reilly Architectural, doors and windows
Hyde Park Mouldings, plasterwork
Dean Barger Studios, decorative painting
Carl Kelley and Terry Stanley, wood hand-carving
The Nanz Company; D.C. Mitchell,
custom door hardware

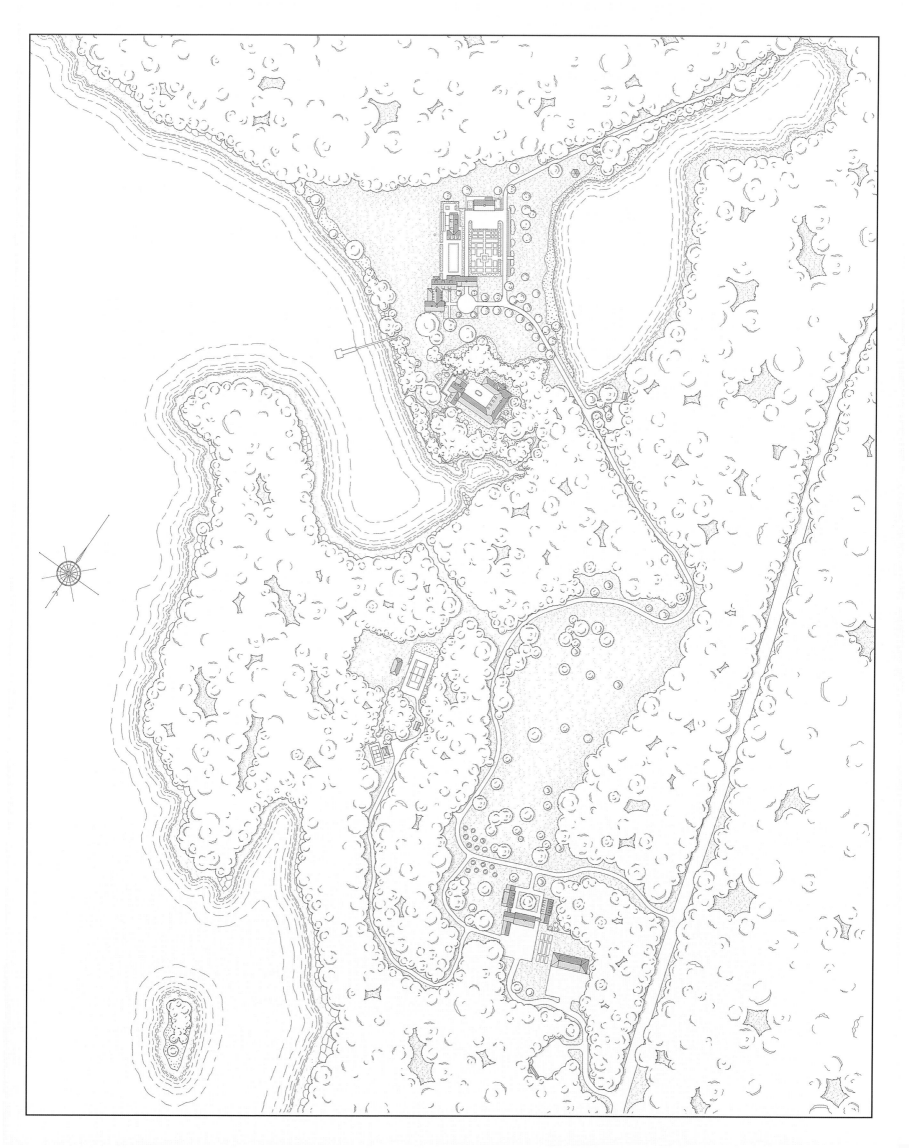

Nantucket, Massachusetts, pages 90–103

Perspective rendering of stair hall in pencil by Brendan McNee

---

F&S TEAM

Oscar Shamamian

Thomas McManus

Stephen Chrisman

Jason Bibens

Andrea Trietsch

Samantha White

Sylvana Gomez
Mendoza

INTERIOR DESIGN

Douglas Durkin Design

LANDSCAPE DESIGN

Julie Jordin Landscapes

CONTRACTOR

Reid Builders

ENGINEERS

SJG Engineering, structural

CES Engineering, mechanical,
electrical, plumbing

ADDITIONAL COLLABORATORS

TBR Marble & Granite, interior stone

Hoff Woodworking; Jutras Woodworking, millwork

Reilly Architectural, doors and windows

Concentric Fabrication, metalwork

Point 618, Inc., decorative painting

E.R. Butler & Co., custom door hardware

Mary Zlot, art consultant

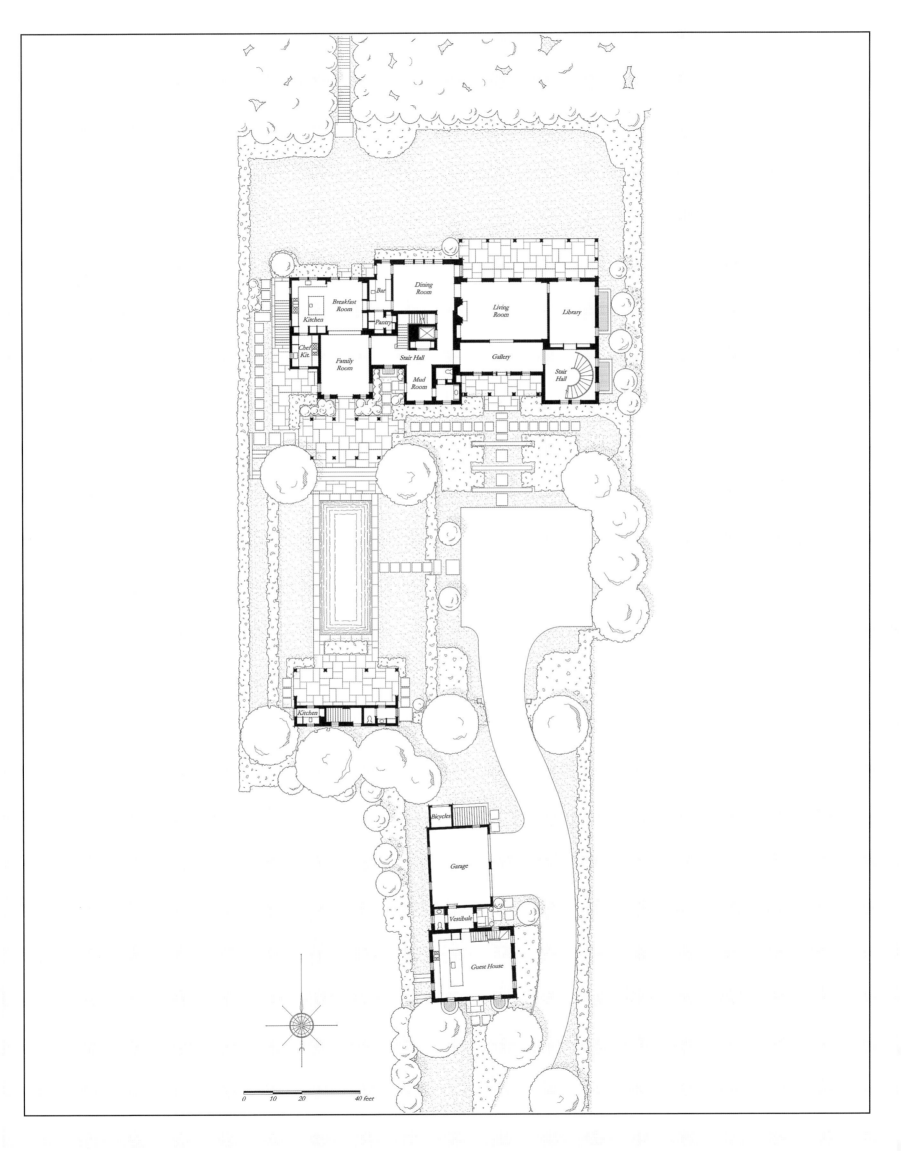

Breakfast Room

Bar

Dining Room

Kitchen

Pantry

Living Room

Library

Chef Kit.

Family Room

Stair Hall

Gallery

Mud Room

Stair Hall

Kitchen

Bicycles

Garage

Vestibule

Guest House

0   10   20   40 feet

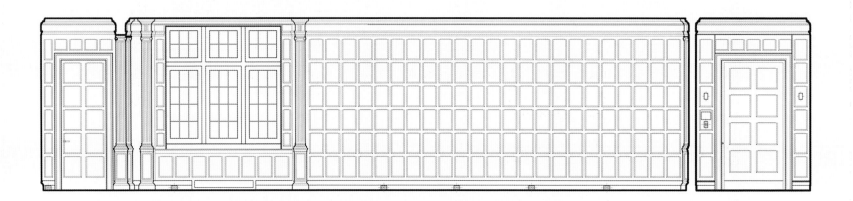

New York, New York, *pages 104–117*

Above: Working drawing of gallery east elevation
Below: Flooring plan of gallery

F&S TEAM
Oscar Shamamian
Andrew Oyen
D'Ann Tollett
Jason Bibens

INTERIOR DESIGN
Jacques Grange

CONTRACTOR
Uberto Construction, Ltd.

ENGINEERS
Silman, structural
CES Engineering, mechanical,
electrical, plumbing

ADDITIONAL COLLABORATORS
Ebenisterie Classique; Catskills Woodworking, millwork
Hyde Park Mouldings, plasterwork
Raredon Resources, metalwork
Precision Stone; Marble Crafters; Voytek Wilk & Co.,
interior stone
Uriu Nuance, decorative painting
H. Theophile, custom door hardware

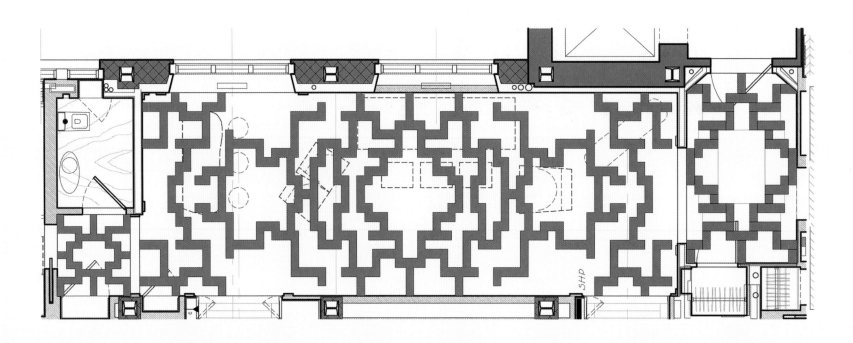

5th Avenue

Dining
Room

Kitchen

Family
Room

Office

Office

Office

Office

Living
Room

Gallery

His
Cl.

Vestibule

Main
Bedroom

Her
Dress.

Bedroom

Bedroom

East 81st Street

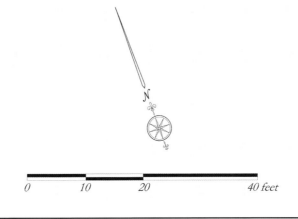

N

0   10   20   40 feet

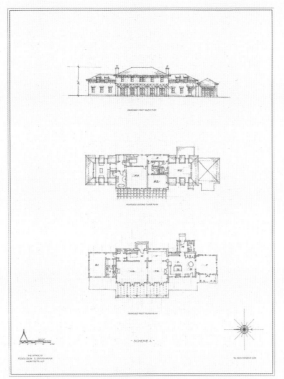
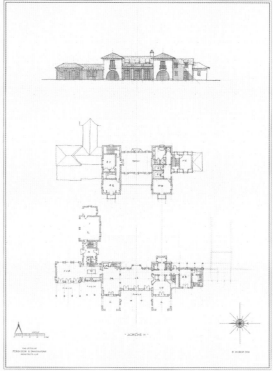
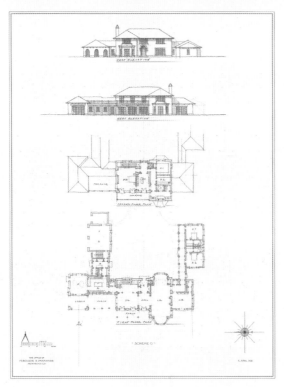
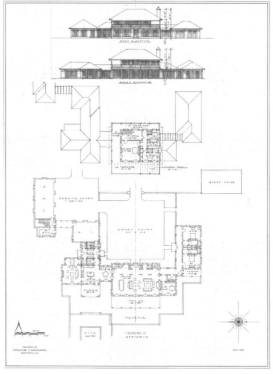

Jupiter Island, Florida, pages 118–131

Hand-drawn elevation and plan studies for schemes A, H, O, and U

F&S TEAM
Oscar Shamamian
Thomas McManus
Stephen Chrisman
Lauren Mitchell
Matthew Enquist
Curtis Gibbs
Louise LeGardeur

INTERIOR DESIGN
Victoria Hagan Interiors

LANDSCAPE DESIGN
SMI Landscape Architecture, Inc.

CONTRACTOR
Hedrick Brothers Construction

ENGINEERS
Carmo Engineering Associates,
structural

Wojcieszak & Associates,
mechanical, electrical, plumbing

ADDITIONAL COLLABORATORS
White House Stone, interior stone
Merritt Woodwork, millwork
Zeluck, Inc., doors and windows

His
Office

Living Room

Dining
Room

Bedroom

Butler's
Pantry

Kitchen

Family
Room

Her
Office

Bar

Entry

Bedroom

Mudroom

Laundry

Garage

Tackle
Room

Guest
Suite

Entry

Storage

Staff
Bedroom

Guest
Suite

Staff
Living
Room

0   10   20   40 feet

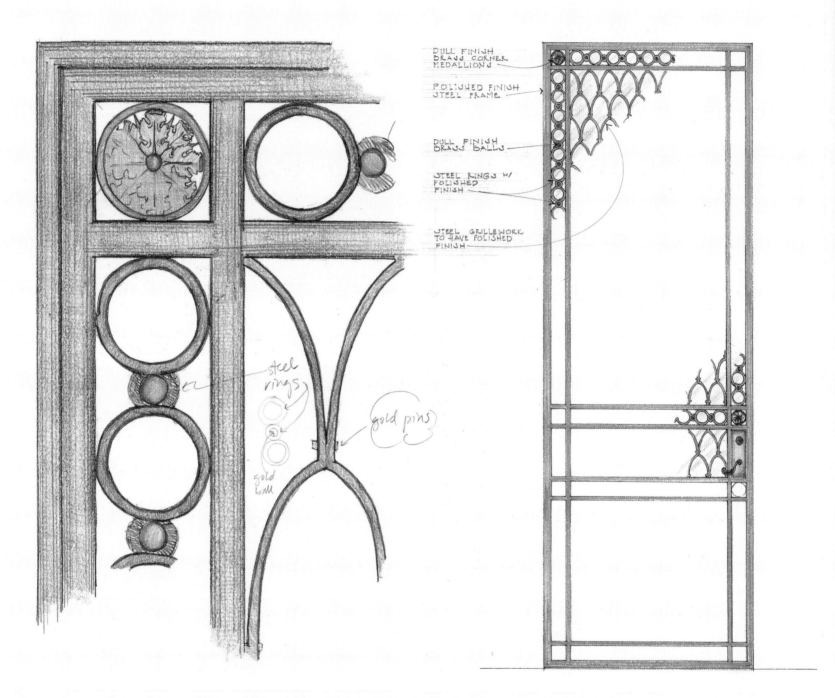

Labels on drawing:
DULL FINISH BRASS CORNER MEDALLIONS
POLISHED FINISH STEEL FRAME
DULL FINISH BRASS BALLS
STEEL RINGS W/ POLISHED FINISH
STEEL GRILLEWORK TO HAVE POLISHED FINISH

steel rings
gold pins
gold ball

New York, New York, pages 136–149

Study of front door in colored pencil by Randy Soprano

F&S TEAM	INTERIOR DESIGN	ENGINEERS	ADDITIONAL COLLABORATORS
Oscar Shamamian	Parish-Hadley Associates and	IP Group, mechanical,	Puccio Marble & Onyx; Precision Stone, interior stone
Courtney Coleman	Brian Murphy, Inc.	electrical, plumbing	Eisenhardt Mills, millwork
Stephen Piersanti			Hope's Windows, windows and doors
Randy Soprano	**CONTRACTOR**		Les Métalliers Champenois, metal and glass doors
	Avatar Construction Inc.		Robert Hoven, decorative painting

East 67th Street

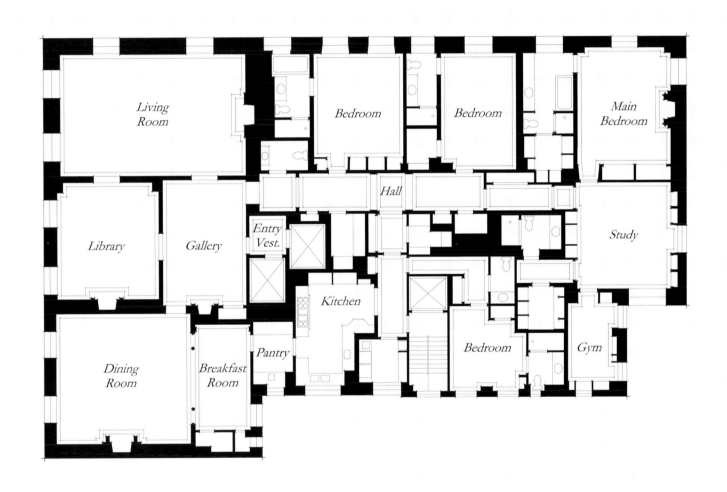

Fifth Avenue

Living Room

Bedroom

Bedroom

Main Bedroom

Library

Gallery

Entry Vest.

Hall

Study

Kitchen

Dining Room

Breakfast Room

Pantry

Bedroom

Gym

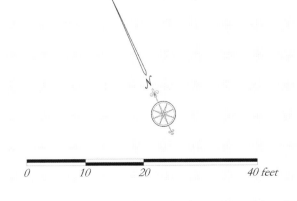

N

0   10   20   40 feet

New York, New York, pages 150–167

Perspective rendering of wine room in pencil by Arthur Dutton

---

F&S TEAM
Oscar Shamamian
Andrew Oyen
Jonathan Hogg
Jennifer Sobol Melone
Andrea Trietsch
Laura Welsh
Rhea Bosland

INTERIOR DESIGN
Haynes-Roberts, Inc.

CONTRACTOR
Lico Contracting, Inc.

ENGINEER
CES Engineering,
mechanical, electrical, plumbing

ADDITIONAL COLLABORATORS
St-One, interior stone
Eisenhardt Mills, millwork
Hope's Windows, windows and doors
Hyde Park Mouldings, plasterwork
Kern/Rockenfield, metalwork
Mead & Josipovich, metal and lacquer front doors
Uriu Nuance, decorative painting
H. Theophile, custom door hardware

East 67th Street

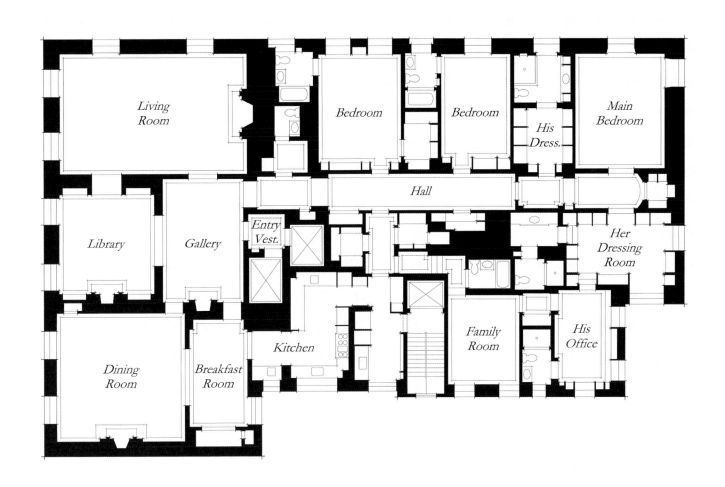

Fifth Avenue

Living Room

Bedroom

Bedroom

His Dress.

Main Bedroom

Hall

Library

Gallery

Entry Vest.

Her Dressing Room

Dining Room

Breakfast Room

Kitchen

Family Room

His Office

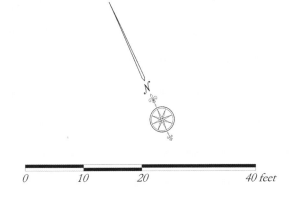

N

0   10   20   40 feet

Greenwich, Connecticut, pages 168–179

Early perspective rendering of rear façade; base drawing by Arthur Dutton
and rendered in colored pencil by Joseph Zvejnieks

F&S TEAM
Oscar Shamamian
Stephen Chrisman
Benjamin Hatherell
Jonathan Hogg
Richard Williams
Ryan Inman
Danielle Potts
Michael Juckiewicz

INTERIOR DESIGN
Victoria Hagan Interiors

LANDSCAPE DESIGN
Kathryn Herman Design and
James Doyle Design Associates

CONTRACTOR
The Tallman Building
Company, Inc.

ENGINEERS
David E. Seymour Engineering,
structural
Tucker Associates, mechanical,
electrical, plumbing

ADDITIONAL COLLABORATORS
Michael Bauro Masonry, masonry
Fairfield County Millwork; Weston Mill Co., millwork
KSD Custom Wood Products, doors and windows
Hyde Park Mouldings, plasterwork
Artistic Iron Works, metalwork
Alfred H. Denninger, weather vane

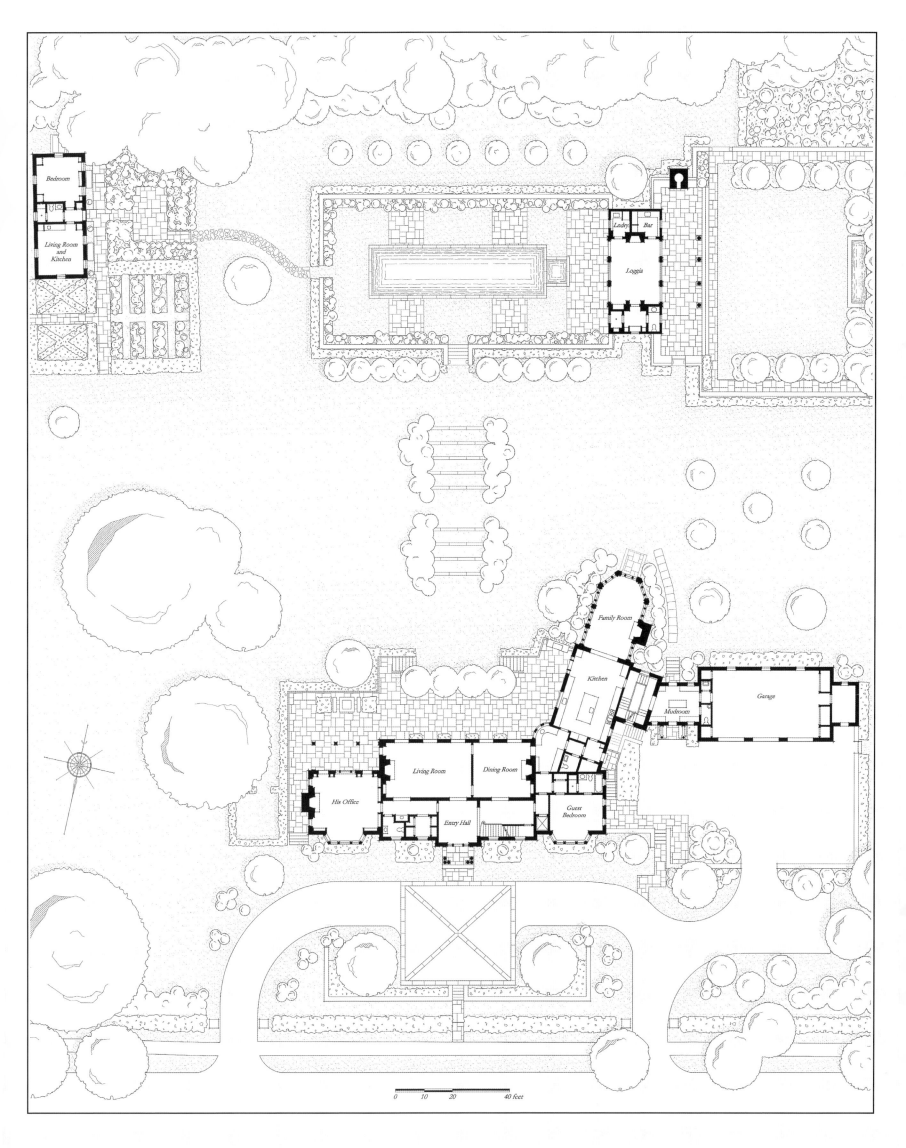

Bedroom

Living Room
and
Kitchen

Lndry | Bar

Loggia

Family Room

Kitchen

Garage

Mudroom

Living Room

Dining Room

His Office

Entry Hall

Guest
Bedroom

0   10   20   40 feet

Bel Air, California, pages 180–193

Below: Mosaic design for inset floor in foyer in colored pencil by Katharine Sandberg
Following spread: Perspective watercolor rendering of entry court by Joseph Zvejnieks

---

F&S TEAM
Mark Ferguson
Scott Sottile
Kristina Mosco
Katharine Sandberg
Tod Elliot
Jennifer Pynn

ASSOCIATE ARCHITECT
Kovac Design Studio

INTERIOR DESIGN
Madeline Stuart & Associates

LANDSCAPE DESIGN
James Doyle Design Associates

CONTRACTOR
MG Partners

ENGINEERS
Soly Yamini and Associates,
structural
California Energy Designs,
mechanical and plumbing
Buratti & Associates, electrical

ADDITIONAL COLLABORATORS
Paul Martin Tile and Stone, masonry
Silver Strand, Inc., millwork
Steelworks Etc., glass and steel windows and doors
Rex J. Pratt, stuc pierre and marmarino plasterwork
Perez Brothers Iron Works, ornamental metalwork
Maria Trimbell, decorative painting
Marmi, floor mosaics
Pashupatina, custom door hardware

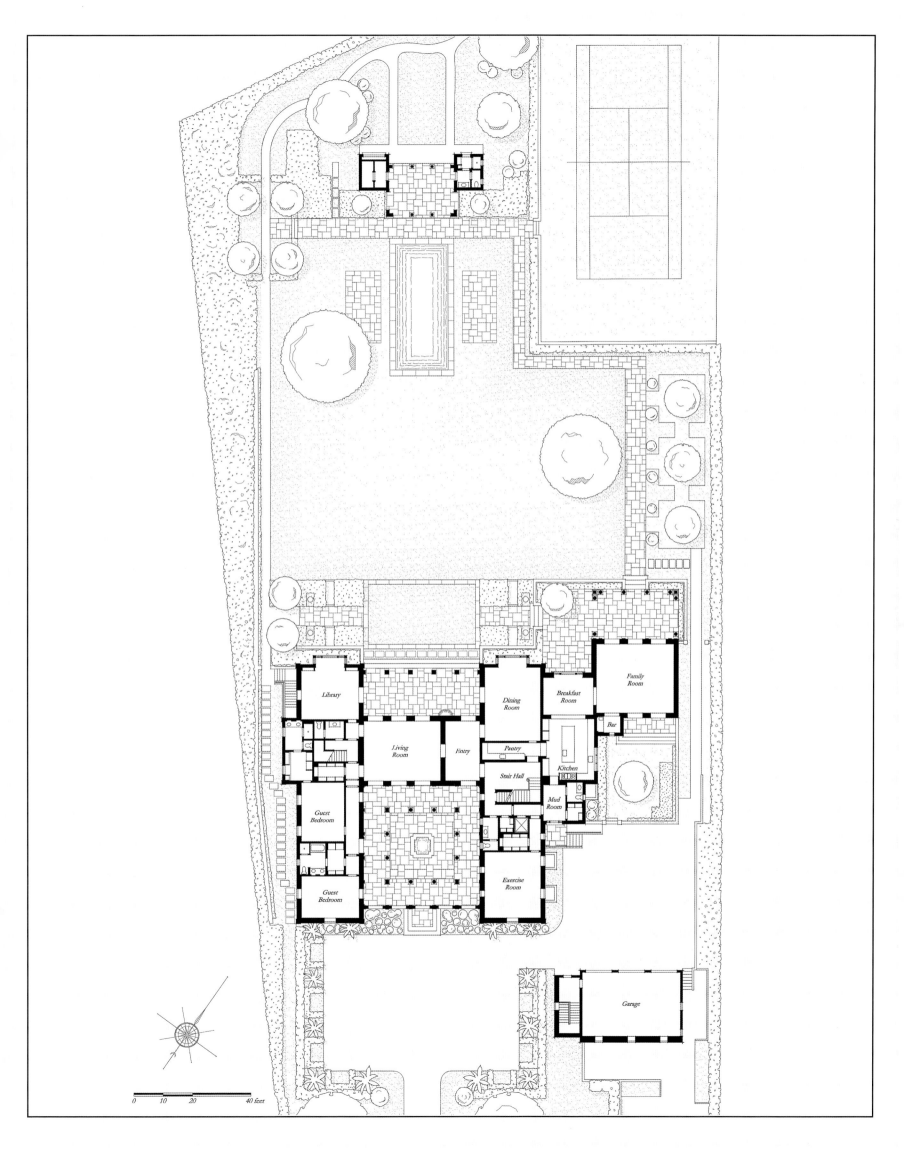

Library

Dining
Room

Breakfast
Room

Family
Room

Living
Room

Entry

Pantry

Bar

Stair Hall

Kitchen

Guest
Bedroom

Mud
Room

Guest
Bedroom

Exercise
Room

Garage

0   10   20   40 feet

Aspen, Colorado, pages 194–207

Perspective rendering of south façade in pencil by Joseph Zvejnieks

---

F&S TEAM
Mark Ferguson
M. Damian Samora
Scott Reinthaler
Alexandra VanOrsdale
Elizabeth Duffy
Josef Albert

ASSOCIATE ARCHITECT
Charles Cunniffe Architects

INTERIOR DESIGN
Bunny Williams Interior Design

LANDSCAPE DESIGN
Design Workshop

CONTRACTOR
Hansen Construction, Inc.

ENGINEERS
Studio NYL; Myers &
Company, structural
Architectural Engineering
Consultants, mechanical,
electrical, plumbing

ADDITIONAL COLLABORATORS
The Gallegos Corporation, masonry
Fraser Woods; Blue Ox Crafters, timbers
Renaissance Works, timber finish
Freedom Metals, metalwork
DG Construction, plasterwork

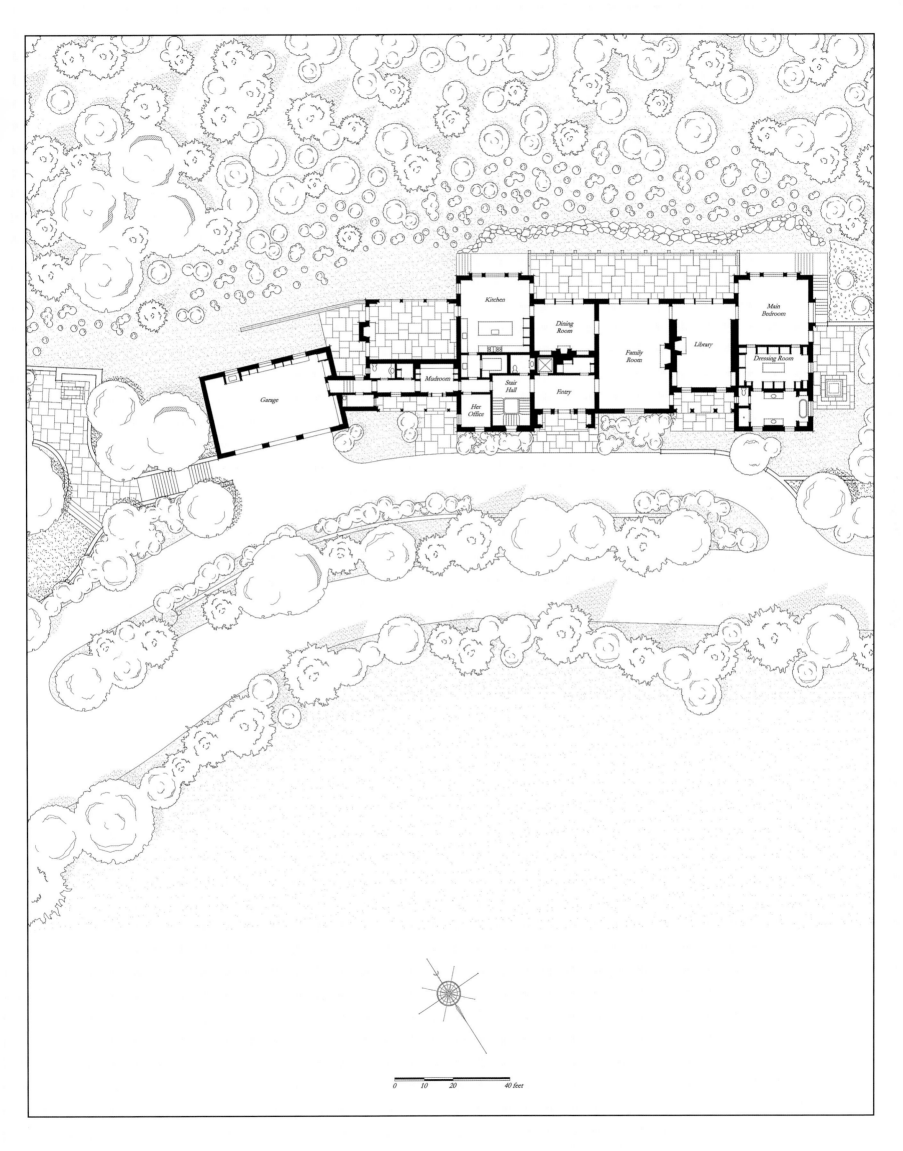

Kitchen

Dining
Room

Main
Bedroom

Family
Room

Library

Mudroom

Dressing Room

Garage

Her
Office

Stair
Hall

Entry

0   10   20   40 feet

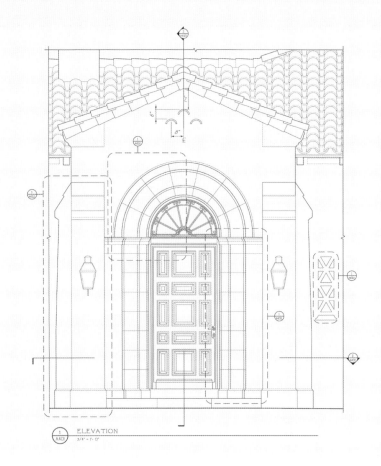

Palm Beach, Florida, *pages 208–223*

Above: Working drawing of front entrance of main house
Below: Perspective rendering of main house in watercolor by Brendan McNee

---

F&S TEAM
Mark Ferguson
Natalie Jacobs
Kristina Mosco
Scott Reinthaler
Luis Almeida
Joseph Mancino
Race Alexander

INTERIOR DESIGN
Bunny Williams Interior Design

LANDSCAPE DESIGN
Nievera Williams Landscape Architecture

CONTRACTOR
Livingston Builders, Inc.

ENGINEERS
Silman, structural
CES Engineering, mechanical, electrical, plumbing

ADDITIONAL COLLABORATORS
Merritt Woodwork, millwork
Peetz Windows and Doors, windows and doors
Hyde Park Mouldings, plasterwork
Reich Metals, metalwork
CV Design, coquina masonry
Fire Features, custom fire baskets

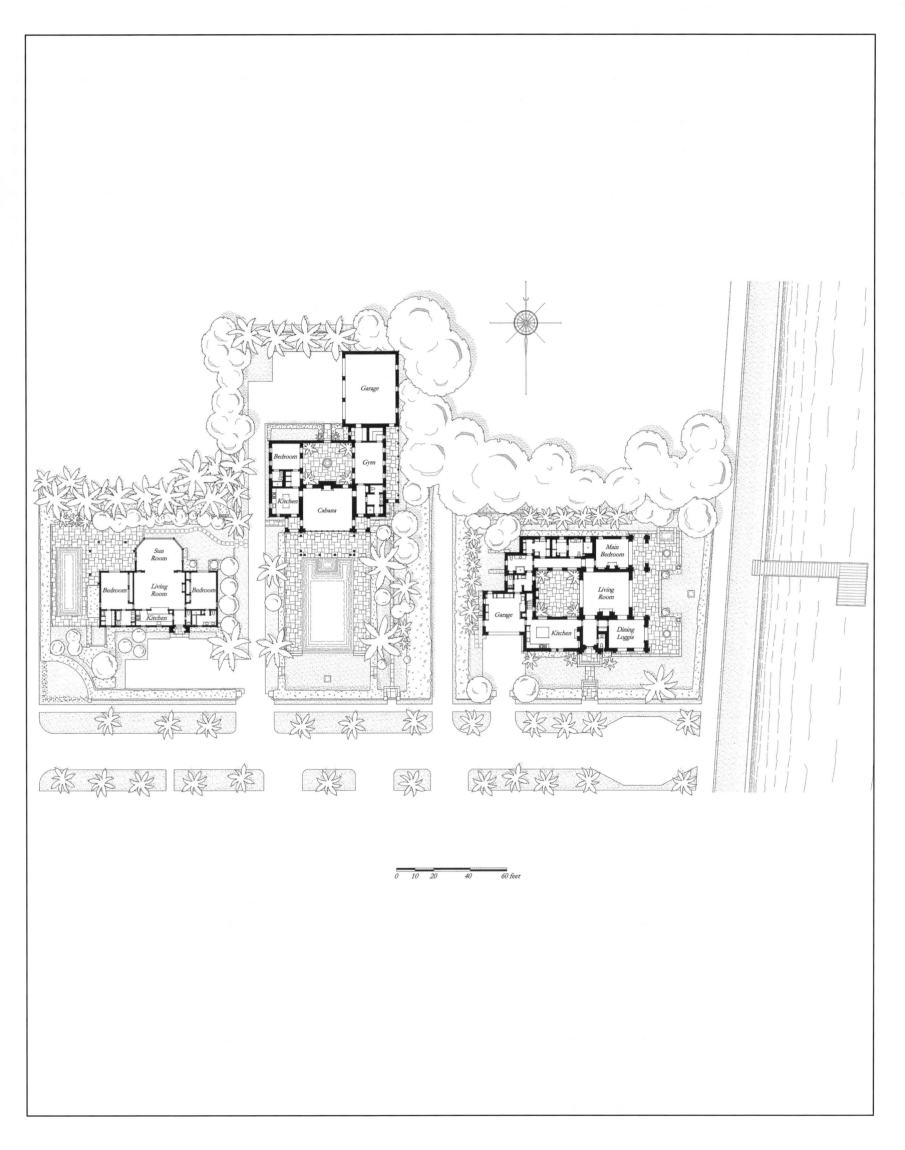

Bedroom

Sun
Room

Living
Room

Bedroom

Kitchen

Garage

Bedroom

Gym

Kitchen

Cabana

Main
Bedroom

Living
Room

Garage

Kitchen

Dining
Loggia

0   10   20   40   60 feet

Fairfield, Connecticut, pages 224–248

Above: Perspective rendering of main house forecourt in pencil by Joseph Zvejnieks
Below: Front elevation of the barn digitally rendered by Brendan McNee

---

F&S TEAM
Oscar Shamamian
Andrew Oyen
Jonathan Hogg
D'Ann Tollett
Scott Porter
Nikita Chabra
Jordan Kasperson
Cindy Michel
Marc Rehman

INTERIOR DESIGN
Tino Zervudachi LLC

LANDSCAPE DESIGN
Miranda Brooks Landscape
Design

**EQUESTRIAN
ARCHITECT**
Blackburn Architects, P.C.

CONTRACTOR
Livingston Builders, Inc.

ENGINEERS
Silman, structural
CES Engineering, mechanical,
electrical, plumbing

ADDITIONAL COLLABORATORS
North Stone Landscaping, masonry
Precision Stone, interior stonework
Architectural Timber and Millwork, beams and timbers
Merritt Woodwork, millwork
Hyde Park Mouldings, plasterwork
The Iron Shop, metalwork
Manuela Zervudachi, decorative metalwork
Frozen Music; Gregory Muller Associates, mosaic work
Uriu Nuance, decorative painting
E.R. Butler & Co.; P.E. Guerin, custom door
and cabinet hardware

0   50   100   200   300 feet

ACKNOWLEDGMENTS

WITH THANKS to our colleagues, every single one of whom fully participate in our demanding work every day. And with thanks to our clients, whose visions are the core of all of our projects; to the interior designers, who collaborate with us on so many aspects of our work and who carry each project to the next level; to the landscape designers, who create the settings and surroundings; to the engineers, without whom our work would not stand up or function properly; to the builders and tradespeople, who build what we draw; and to the artisans and craftspeople, who further the work by creating elements that cannot simply be drawn or designed.

We thank the art and design director of this book, Charles Churchward, who has curated images of our work and guided the way we create atmosphere and whose beautiful presentation has amplified our excitement for each of these projects; Emily Wardwell for her expertise in helping to design and prepare these pages; writer David Masello for his insight, eloquence, and especially for bringing these residences to life by allowing all of the participants to have a voice; Margaret Russell, a great friend of the firm, for her kind words and support, her impeccable taste, and her intimate knowledge of us and all of the players; Andrew Alpern for his scholarship and for reminding us of those who built before us; the photographers, especially Lisa Romerein and Thomas Loof, for seeing our projects in ways that we could not, for their determination and ability to give us what we need (and even more), and for their infinite patience with us; Andrew Frasz for so beautifully capturing both process and results; the stylists, including Mieke ten Have, Howard Christian, and Hoot & Heart Co., who remind us that our projects are homes; and our publisher, Rizzoli International Publications, especially editor Andrea Danese and publisher Charles Miers, for their forbearance in making this monograph happen during this difficult time. We are also grateful to Anthony Amiano and Kate Sandberg for their diligence and meticulousness in putting all the pieces together; and to Andrés Blanco, whose passion for this book helped us immeasurably.

We and everyone at the firm thank our families, partners, and friends for their patience and tolerance of the long hours required to create these projects and this monograph.

Finally, we all wish to express our utmost appreciation to Mark Ferguson and Oscar Shamamian for their expertise and counsel, which helped make this book a reality; for their leadership, mentorship, guidance, and trust every day; and for starting and building this firm for the benefit of all of us.

—*NINA BRANSFIELD, Senior Associate–Director of Marketing & ANDREW OYEN, Principal*

Opposite: In an apartment at 2 East 67th Street, a long hall is punctuated by a paneled dome supported by fluted pilasters. *Above*: A refurbished British phone booth is the clandestine entrance to the playhouse nightclub in Maine.

CONTRIBUTORS

DAVID MASELLO is executive editor of *Milieu* magazine. Masello has previously held senior editorial positions at such magazines as *Travel + Leisure*, *Art & Antiques*, *Departures*, *Country Living*, and *Town & Country*. A noted writer on culture and art, his work has appeared in the *New York Times*, *Wall Street Journal*, *Fine Art Connoisseur*, and *Best American Essays*, as well as in literary magazines. He is the author of *Architecture without Rules: The Houses of Marcel Breuer and Herbert Beckhard* and *Art in Public Places*. He is a board member of and frequent performer for Read650.org.

MARGARET RUSSELL is a design journalist and consultant who was formerly the editor in chief of *Elle Decor* and *Architectural Digest*.

ANDREW ALPERN is an architectural historian, architect, and attorney. An expert on historic apartment houses, he has authored many books on the subject.

CHARLES CHURCHWARD is an art and design director who, during his nearly forty-year career, has worked for such publications as *Vogue*, *Vanity Fair*, and *House & Garden*, as well as contributed to the *New York Times' Magazine*, *Mademoiselle*, and *Ms.* magazines. Churchward has authored and designed numerous books, including *Herb Ritts: The Golden Hour*; *It's Modern*; *Vogue Living*; and *A Peculiar Paradise*.

A mosaic backsplash crafted by Frozen Music
for a kitchen in Connecticut includes the French proverb
La table est l'entremetteuse de l'amitié.

Previous spread: A pergola at a pool
house in Connecticut.

Right: In East Hampton, looking
toward the guesthouse from
the front door of the main house.

First published in the United States of America in 2021
By Rizzoli International Publications, Inc.
300 Park Avenue South
New York, NY 10010
www.rizzoliusa.com

Text by David Masello
Foreword by Margaret Russell
For photography credits, see page 282

Design by Charles Churchward

For Rizzoli International Publications:
Publisher: Charles Miers
Editor: Andrea Danese
Production: Alyn Evans

Printed in Hong Kong

2021 2022 2023 2024 2025 / 10 9 8 7 6 5 4 3 2 1

ISBN: 978-0-8478-7060-8
Library of Congress Control Number: 2021937530

Visit us online:
Facebook.com/RizzoliNewYork
Twitter: @Rizzoli_Books
Instagram.com/RizzoliBooks
Pinterest.com/RizzoliBooks
Youtube.com/user/RizzoliNY
Issuu.com/Rizzoli

286

F&S